THE MISTRY DYNASTY: HERITAGE AND HOME

Kerfegar Mistry

ABOUT THE AUTHOR

I'm Kerfegar Mistry, a writer shaped by the rich tapestry of my Parsi heritage and the stories that have been passed down through generations of my family. Growing up in Nasik, our ancestral home was more than just a place to live, it was a witness to laughter, love, and the everyday magic of life. That house, with its creaking floors and dusty drawers, sparked my love for storytelling and inspired me to preserve the legacy of those who came before me.

By nature, I'm a quiet and reflective person, preferring to observe and absorb the world around me. Writing has always been my way of expressing what I find difficult to say aloud, a way to connect with others and share the deeply personal moments that shape us all. "The Mistry Dynasty: Heritage and Home" is my heartfelt attempt to capture the essence of my family's history, weaving together nostalgia, love, and the enduring importance of home.

When I'm not writing, you'll likely find me enjoying a cup of English Tea, reflecting on life's little joys, or spending time with the people who matter most to me. This book is a labor of love, and it's my way of inviting you into the world that shaped me. I hope it resonates with you as much as it has with me.

Dedication

A Letter to My Beloved Family

Every family has its storyteller, the keeper of memories who breathes life into the tales of the past. In our family, I proudly take on that role. I have always loved stories, the way they can transport us, teach us, and connect us to something larger than ourselves. But this isn't about the stories I tell; it's about the story I live every day, my own.

I've always been someone who cherishes the little things in life. I find joy in moments, whether it's the aroma of fresh ink on paper or the laughter of my family. As I sit down to write these words, I am overwhelmed with a sense of gratitude, love, and pride for the family that has shaped my life in ways too profound to express. This book is my humble attempt to capture the essence of who we are, where we come from, and the incredible legacy that has been passed down through the generations. It is not just a recounting of history but a celebration of the bonds we share, the lessons we've learned, and the stories that make us who we are.

This book is about us. It is about the vision of Jamsetjee Nowrojee, who laid the foundation of our family business in 1847, and about Shirinbai Banaji, whose resilience and ingenuity saw us through the darkest times. It is about Fuiji's laughter, the mischief of Minoo kaka, the challenges faced by Baapi and Bawa, and the triumphs that have defined our journey as a family. It is about the grand white house that stands as a symbol of our history and the business that has been our lifeblood, weathering storms of prohibition, bans, and even pandemics.

—

You will find in these pages the mischievous tales of Polly Kaka, Mehernosh kaka and my dad Darayus. You will read about the sacrifices made, the love shared, and the legacy preserved through generations. It is a tapestry woven with the threads of laughter, determination, and boundless affection. This book is also deeply personal. It is my story, too, and a reflection of how all of you have influenced the person I am today. This book is my way of honoring you all, my family, and expressing the profound impact you've had on my life. And this, my dear family, is just the first of the many books I have written so far. Each one, in its own way, carries a part of our story and a piece of my heart.

I must also acknowledge the incredible women of our family, whose strength, grace, and love have been the bedrock of our legacy. Rati Kaki, with her wisdom and nurturing presence, has always been the family advisor imparting knowledge, offering guidance and love at every step. Mahrukh Kaki, with her vivacious spirit and unparalleled kindness, has shown us what it means to embrace life with open arms and unwavering generosity. And my mother, Hutoxi, the youngest daughter-in-law of the family, has been a true beacon of love, dedication, and resilience. Each of them has contributed immensely to our family's story, teaching us the importance of compassion, unity, and perseverance.

A special mention must go to my incredible sisters, Benaifer, Yasmin, Sanaya, and Del-ara. Each of them has brought unique joy and wisdom into my life. Benaifer, with her grace and calm demeanor, has always been a pillar of support. Yasmin, whose laughter can light up any room, reminds me to find happiness in the simplest things. Sanaya, with her fierce determination and kindness, has taught me the value of compassion and perseverance.

And Del-ara, my closest companion in life's adventures, has been my partner in crime, my confidante, and my source of endless inspiration. Each of them has played a vital role in shaping who I am today, and this book is as much a celebration of their love and guidance as it is of our family's legacy.

As you turn these pages, I hope you find yourself smiling, reminiscing, and feeling the warmth of the memories, we've created together. This book is not just a story; it is a love letter to each of you, a reminder of how lucky we are to share this journey. Thank you for being my strength, my inspiration, and my constant support. This book is as much yours as it is mine.

With all my love,
Lord Kerfegar Mistry

INDEX

Chapter 1: The House That Built a Family

The Mistry bungalow is more than just a structure; it is a storyteller, silently narrating tales of a century gone by. Its towering arches and sturdy pillars stand witness to the lives, joys, and sorrows of generations of my family. An aura of mystery and history surrounds this house, especially when we talk about its origins. Family lore tells us that the bungalow was built in 1909. While we lack documented evidence to confirm this, old Manek, my father's aunt firmly believed it to be true. In her later years, she would often remind us, "This grand house has stood strong for generations." It became a family marker, a milestone we quietly celebrated as yet another testament to the endurance of our roots.

The name "Mistry" holds its own significance in this story. Derived from the Gujarati word for "craftsman" or "architect," it feels almost predestined that the Mistry bungalow would become a paragon of architectural brilliance. Perhaps this name reflected the very essence of my great-grandfather Banaji, the man who, as family legend suggests, was not only the house's owner but also its original designer. Banaji's work on the house was not just about bricks and mortar, it was about vision and meticulousness. Every element of the bungalow speaks of a craftsman's dedication and artistry. The entrance is grand yet welcoming, a portal to a world of elegance and tradition. The wide veranda wraps around the house, a perfect space for morning tea and family conversations.

But the most striking feature of the house is the open passage in the middle, a rare design choice that brings light and air to the very heart of the home. This design allowed the family to gather under an open sky, even within the confines of the bungalow.

The arches and old styled roof were built to stand the test of time, and their timeless beauty is evident even today. "Banaji must have poured his soul into this house," my father once told me. "Every detail, every corner, reflects care and precision."

Over the years, the house has been more than just a home; it has been the nucleus of the Mistry family. It has witnessed the full spectrum of human experiences, births that brought joy and hope, weddings that created new alliances, and deaths that left us in mourning. This was the house where my great-grandparents Shirinbai and Banaji began their married life, raising their three children under its roof. It was here that my grandmother Silloo came as a young bride to start a new chapter with my grandfather Jamshed. It was where countless Navroz celebrations were held, filling the halls with the aroma of traditional Parsi cuisine and the laughter of multiple generations.

The bungalow has also stood tall during pivotal moments in history. It weathered the storms of colonial rule, India's fight for independence, the prohibition years, world wars, COVID-19 and the dawn of a new nation. Through wars and societal transformations, its walls remained a sanctuary, offering stability and hope to the family within, even as the world outside changed drastically.

The bungalow's unique charm lies in its ability to adapt and evolve. It has worn many hats over the years, serving as more than just a family home. At one point, a portion of the house was leased to a bank, its rooms filled with the shuffle of papers and the hum of clerks at work. Another time, it operated as a post office, connecting people and stories across the region.

The house was also transformed into a guesthouse, where travelers were treated to warm hospitality, with meals lovingly prepared as if they were family. Additionally, it once served as a hotel called The Nasik Hotel, welcoming guests from far and wide, providing them with comfort and a sense of belonging in its quaint and charming setting.

Beyond its roles in business and hospitality, the house also became a place of refuge in times of crisis. Since haystacks were often stored nearby, fires would sometimes break out, engulfing entire sections of the Ganjmal area in flames. During these terrifying moments, people would rush to our house for shelter while firefighters battled to control the blaze. The thick walls and open verandahs provided safety, and within those walls, fear-stricken families found solace, waiting for the flames to subside.

The bungalow also became a cherished wedding venue for many people around the city, hosting celebrations filled with joy, music, and laughter. Its spacious halls and serene surroundings made it an ideal location for such memorable occasions. In fact, my father's teacher, held a Catholic wedding in this very house, adding a touch of personal history to its already storied past. The house stood as a witness to vows exchanged, uniting families and creating moments to be treasured for generations.

Perhaps one of the most unusual and unexpected chapters in the history of this bungalow is when it became home to a group of German circus performers who had brought their traveling show to Nashik City. The circus was set up near the Golf Club, drawing crowds from all over, but what was even more fascinating was that the performers themselves took up residence in our very house.

—

Among them was not just a troupe of skilled acrobats, jugglers, and entertainers but also an unexpected and rather peculiar guest—a chimpanzee! Yes, you read that right. A Chimpanzee! Imagine a chimpanzee living within these very walls, moving through the house as if it were just another member of the family. This chimpanzee, highly trained and disciplined, was not just a passive houseguest. It actively participated in daily household activities.

One of its most astonishing talents was its ability to clear the dining table after meals. As soon as everyone was done eating, the chimpanzee would swiftly gather the used dishes, carefully balancing them in its small hands, and take them to the kitchen for washing. It was a sight both amusing and incredible, a trained circus animal seamlessly fitting into domestic life. While most of the family marveled at this spectacle, not everyone found it endearing. Shirinbai, in particular, was absolutely terrified of the chimpanzee. She would go out of her way to avoid crossing paths with it, often retreating into another room whenever it entered. The idea of a primate casually roaming about the house was simply too much for her to bear.

Shirinbai was also deeply concerned that the chimpanzee, with its small but strong hands, would drop and break the delicate plates while clearing the table. She would often watch nervously from a distance, wincing at every movement, expecting a crash at any moment. But to her astonishment, the chimpanzee never broke a single plate. It handled the dishes with remarkable care, as if it knew exactly how fragile they were. Over time, even though she remained wary of the animal, she had to grudgingly admit that it was incredibly well-trained.

Interestingly, this unusual chapter of our house's history also left a lasting impression on my dad's uncle, Minoo uncle. Spending time around the circus performers, he became fascinated by their skills and would often watch them train. It is believed that his later passion for juggling was inspired by these early interactions. He would mimic their tricks, practicing tirelessly, and eventually became quite adept at the art. The influence of the circus, in this way, extended beyond just the temporary guests, it left behind skills and stories that would be passed down through generations.

The image of a chimpanzee scurrying through the halls, Shirinbai gasping in horror as it casually picked up dishes, and Minoo Kaka learning the art of juggling from the circus troupe paints a picture of a house that has seen truly extraordinary moments. This bungalow has always been a place of fascinating encounters, where the unexpected becomes part of the home's very fabric. And for a brief period, it was a place where the boundaries between a family home and a traveling circus blurred, creating memories that remain alive in our stories to this day.

Now, let me take you on a journey to uncover the extraordinary story of my great-grandparents, Shirinbai and Banaji, whose legacy not only shaped our family but also laid the foundation for businesses that would thrive across generations. It all began with a fateful moment when young Shirinbai arrived in Nasik, seeking treatment at the local sanatorium at Deolali, due to health complications. Having made the long journey all the way from Surat, she could never have known that this trip would set in motion a life-changing encounter. It was here, in the serene surroundings of the sanatorium, that she met Banaji.

Banaji, a man with a strong sense of purpose and vision, was drawn to Shirinbai's grace and resilience. What began as a chance conversation soon blossomed into something far deeper, an undeniable connection that neither of them could ignore. Their bond grew stronger with each passing day, and what seemed like a fleeting moment in time turned into a lifelong partnership. In fact, it was in the very bungalow where they had met that their love story truly began to take shape, as they eventually exchanged vows and began a new chapter of life together.

At the time, Shirinbai was a young bride, full of hope and dreams, stepping into a future she could not yet envision. Banaji, a man of vision and ambition, stood beside her, and together they created something extraordinary. They help build Jamsetjee Nowrojee & Co, one of the oldest and most respected liquor enterprises in the city, a business that would become a cornerstone of our family legacy. Over time, their names became synonymous with success, and the company was eventually renamed Shirinbai Banaji Mistry & Sons, a fitting tribute to their partnership and enduring strength.

However, their story was not without its hardships. Tragedy struck when Banaji passed away unexpectedly at a young age, leaving Shirinbai not only with the immense responsibility of running the business but also the daunting task of raising three young children, Minoo, Manek, and Jamshed. In an era when widows were often pushed to the margins of society, my great-grandmother chose a path of defiance and resilience. She didn't just survive; she thrived. These words echoed in my mind as I grew older, and the true extent of her strength, resilience, and unwavering determination became clearer with time. Her legacy, one of love, ambition, and sheer grit, continues to inspire us all.

Among her children, Jamshed, my grandfather, stepped up to assist her. From a young age, he was by her side, learning the intricacies of the business and absorbing the values of hard work and integrity that would define him for the rest of his life. Minoo, the eldest child, was bold and more inclined toward intellectual pursuits. He helped with business and offered sage advice whenever needed. Manek, the only daughter, brought a sense of lightness to the household with her lively spirit. Silloo, my grandmother, also played a significant role in the business. She managed the cash counter with precision and diligently took care of clerical responsibilities. Together, they formed a cohesive team that kept the business and the house thriving, each bringing their unique strengths to the table.

Manek and Minoo never married. Instead, they dedicated their lives to the family, becoming the anchors that kept the Mistry name strong. They were known for their wisdom and compassion, always ready to lend a hand or an ear.

Jamshed, however, carried the torch forward in a different way. He married my grandmother, Silloo, and together, they began a new chapter for the family. Though I was too young to remember them clearly, their presence loomed large in the stories I grew up hearing. My father described Jamshed as a shy and reserved man, someone who spoke little but whose actions spoke volumes. Silloo, on the other hand, was known for her fiery spirit and short temper, a woman who commanded respect and kept everyone on their toes. Despite their contrasting personalities, they complemented each other, creating a dynamic partnership that left a lasting legacy in both the family and the business.

Silloo and Jamshed had three sons, Parvez, Mehernosh, and my father, Darayus. All three completely different and unique in their own ways. Together, they carried forward the Mistry legacy, each finding their own way to contribute to the family's success.

Parvez, the eldest, was the first to venture into new territory. With Jamshed's guidance, he established KitKat, a general store that quickly became a beloved fixture in the community.
Mehernosh, the middle son, followed in his father's footsteps, setting up another store called Mistry Liquor Mart, the oldest liquor store in Nasik Road. He, along with my grandfather Jamshed operated and managed that store onto brilliance.
My father, Darayus, took over the family business, S.B. Mistry & Sons, all three brothers ensuring that the cornerstone of our legacy remained strong.

Silloo played a pivotal role in these transitions, not just raising her sons but also finding them partners who would complement their ambitions. My mother, Hutoxi and aunts Rati and Mahrukh often spoke of how they were welcomed into the family with open arms, encouraged to contribute their talents and strengths to the household and its enterprises. How each of my aunts were terrified of Silloo but still knew the love she shared among them.

Growing up, I was captivated by this bungalow's secrets. Locked rooms, dusty trunks, and forgotten corners seemed to whisper untold stories. My favorite spot was the veranda, where the family would gather in the evenings. The Mistry bungalow has aged gracefully, its walls bearing the patina of time. Cracks have appeared in places, and some sections have needed repairs, but its essence remains unchanged.

It continues to be the heart of the family, a place where past and present coexist.

Every family gathering feels like a reunion not just of people but of history itself. Stories flow freely. Each anecdote adds another layer to the house's rich narrative. As I walk through the bungalow today, I am struck by its enduring spirit. It is more than just a structure; it is a testament to the resilience and ingenuity of the Mistry's.
For me, it is a place of inspiration, a reminder of the legacy I am fortunate to be a part of. This house, with its arches and tall roof, its open passage and sprawling veranda, is not just the heart of the Mistry family, it is the soul of our story. And as long as it stands, so too will the memories and values that define us.

Chapter 2: Jamsetjee Nowrojee & Co.

The origins of the family business date back to 1847, when it was first established under the name Jamsetjee Nowrojee and Co. However, the true story behind its name and its founder remains a mystery to this day. We don't really know why the shop was named after Jamsetjee Nowrojee, who he was, or how he is related to our family. That information has been lost over generations, tucked away in the annals of our ancestors' lives. Some say that years ago, there were two partners who ran the business, but they eventually separated, leaving the Mistry family with the responsibility of continuing the enterprise. Others believe the business originally started in Mumbai and was later moved to Nasik. There's also a tale that this business was a gift given to the man who married the only daughter of the family. Despite these various theories, the true origin of Jamsetjee Nowrojee and Co. remains uncertain, and we may never know the full story behind its creation.

What we do know is that what began as a modest enterprise quickly became an iconic institution in the district. Over the years, the shop gained a reputation that far surpassed its humble beginnings, earning the prestigious distinction of holding Licence No. 1, the very first liquor license ever issued in the entire region. This was a mark of trust and legitimacy, not just for the business but also for the family, cementing its place as a cornerstone of the community and a symbol of reliability in an ever-changing world. Though the origin story may be lost, the legacy of Jamsetjee Nowrojee and Co. lives on in the hearts of those who remember its significance.

Beyond selling alcohol, the family's entrepreneurial spirit led them to expand their ventures further.

The business also served as Agents to The Oriental Government Security Life Assurance Company Ltd, showcasing their versatility and deep integration into the commercial fabric of the region. Additionally, the premises housed operations for the manufacturing and selling of spring water, and even the making and selling of toddy, a testament to the resourcefulness and innovation that defined the family enterprise.

The business operated under its original name for decades before being renamed S.B. Mistry & Sons. This rebranding was in honor of Shirinbai Banaji, the matriarch of the family, whose initials (S.B.) came to represent the values and legacy of the enterprise. The transition marked a new chapter, one that carried forward the spirit of enterprise and determination epitomized by Shirinbai.

The store itself was, and still is, a central feature of the family's ancestral property. Situated at the front of the grand premises, it serves as both a commercial hub and a symbolic link to the family's rich history. The proximity of the shop to the house has always allowed the business and the family to coexist harmoniously, blending the personal with the professional in a way that's uniquely Mistry. From the bustling activity of the store to the tranquil corners of the family home, this harmonious balance between work and life has been a defining characteristic of the family's legacy, one built not only on commerce but also on adaptability, tradition, and pride.

Shirinbai's Leadership
After the passing of Banaji, it was Shirinbai who took the reins of the business. This was no small feat, especially during a time when women in business were a rarity. But Shirinbai, with her indomitable spirit and sharp acumen, rose to the occasion.

She not only managed the day-to-day operations of the store but also ensured that it continued to thrive, providing stability to the family during challenging times. Many relatives from her side of the family came forward to help her run the business and house, but she declined their offers, choosing instead to take care of everything single-handedly.

Her leadership was put to the ultimate test in 1950 when the government imposed a prohibition on alcohol sales. For sixteen long years, from 1950 to 1966, the store was forced to close its doors, leaving the family without its primary source of income.

The closure was not just a financial setback but a blow to the family's identity, as the business had been a cornerstone of their livelihood for decades. Yet, even during this difficult period, Shirinbai's resilience shone through. She found creative ways to make ends meet, ensuring that the family never lacked for essentials. The store, once a bustling hub of activity, stood silent, its shutters down and its shelves gathering dust, a poignant reminder of the challenges the family faced. But Shirinbai never let despair take hold; instead, she focused on navigating these trying times with unwavering determination.

Survival During Prohibition
Faced with the challenge of keeping the household and its sprawling estate afloat, Shirinbai turned to innovation. She transformed the family home into a Bed and Breakfast, welcoming travelers and visitors who sought a warm and hospitable place to stay. The house, with its grand architecture and welcoming atmosphere, became a temporary sanctuary for many during this period. In addition to the Bed and Breakfast, Shirinbai found other creative ways to generate income.

The property was rented out for marriages and cultural programs, bringing life and activity to the estate even during the most trying times.

During the prohibition era, Shirinbai's resourcefulness reached new heights. With the liquor business now off-limits, she seized the opportunity to diversify. She turned part of the estate into a manufacturing unit for "High Class Mountain Spring Water," which she sold to nearby towns and villages. Bottles of crisp, clean water, became a sought-after commodity, quickly gaining a reputation for its purity. But Shirinbai didn't stop there. Alongside the water, she began collecting sap from the region's palm trees to make Toddy, a mildly fermented drink beloved by locals. This small yet clever venture allowed her to continue supporting the family and the estate during a period of significant hardship.

The house itself also served as a post office and a bank, further cementing its role as a vital part of the community. These initiatives not only ensured the financial stability of the family but also preserved the legacy of the property as a place of service and community engagement. Shirinbai's efforts during this period were nothing short of heroic. She proved that adversity could be met with resilience and creativity, turning challenges into opportunities.

The Nasik Hotel
One of Shirinbai's most ingenious ventures during the prohibition era was converting the family home into a restaurant, fondly referred to as " The Nasik Hotel." The grand dining hall was transformed into a bustling eatery where guests from all walks of life would gather to enjoy delicious, home-cooked meals. Shirinbai took pride in personally overseeing the kitchen, ensuring that every dish met her exacting standards.

The menu featured a mix of Parsi delicacies, creating a unique blend that kept customers coming back for more. Word quickly spread about the Nasik Hotel, and it became a popular dining spot in the area. Travelers, locals, and even prominent community members would stop by to savor the hearty meals and experience the warm hospitality. The lively chatter of diners, the clinking of cutlery, and the tantalizing aroma of freshly cooked food filled the house, breathing new life into the once-quiet estate. Through the Nasik Hotel, Shirinbai not only provided for her family but also created a space that brought people together, showcasing her ability to turn a family home into a vibrant hub of community and commerce.

The General Provisions Store
During the prohibition era, when the liquor store was forced to close its doors, Shirinbai's ingenuity took center stage. The familiar shop, once filled with the vibrant hum of customers purchasing their favorite spirits, underwent a transformation. She repurposed the space into a General Provisions Store, adapting to the needs of the time. The store was no longer stocked with bottles and barrels of liquor but instead filled with the everyday essentials that the community relied on.

The shelves, which once held fine wines and spirits, now housed neatly stacked bars of soap, cans of kerosene, boxes of biscuits, jars of chocolates, and reams of stationery. The store had a welcoming, almost comforting atmosphere, with the scent of fresh goods mingling with the wooden shelves and the old wooden counter that had seen generations of customers. The walls, once adorned with liquor advertisements, now displayed signs for household goods, offering a stark but necessary change for the community during this difficult time.

In one corner of the store, you could find colorful bottles of soda lemon, orange, and raspberry, which were manufactured in codd neck bottles, also called "Goli Bottles" in India. These were filled with carbonated drinks that brought a sense of refreshment and nostalgia to many. The distinctive shape of the bottles, with their marble stopper sealed tightly inside, added a touch of vintage charm, as customers remembered a simpler time when these fizzy drinks were a beloved treat.

Shirinbai made sure that the store was stocked with everything the locals needed, no matter how small or big the item. She organized the shelves meticulously, every item had its place, ensuring customers could easily find what they needed. The aisles were narrow but orderly, with items in boxes stacked high along the walls. The faint creak of the floor as customers walked around the store was a sound that many would come to know well. Above the shelves, old wooden cabinets stored emergency supplies, and in the corner of the room, a small wooden desk stood where Shirinbai would sometimes sit, greeting each customer with a warm smile or engaging in brief, friendly chats. The General Provisions Store soon became a hub for the local community, where people could gather and exchange stories while picking up their daily supplies. It was a meeting point, a place where news was shared, gossip exchanged, and friendships deepened. The store was often filled with the chatter of relatives and family members who would stop by to help out or simply to check in on Shirinbai, offering support.

On any given day, the store might be bustling with the energy of cousins helping to stock the shelves, uncles and aunts assisting customers, and neighbors popping in for a quick conversation.

It was a gathering spot, not just for business, but for family and community connections.

Shirinbai's careful management of the store kept it well-stocked and running smoothly, but it was her personal touch that made it a beloved institution. She knew the families who came in, their likes, dislikes, and struggles. She would often go out of her way to offer goods on credit to those who were down on their luck, ensuring that no one went without.

And as the store continued to thrive, the whole family rallied behind her, doing their part to ensure the success of the business. These moments of togetherness, amid the hard work, became a cherished tradition, further binding the family and the store to the community they served.

The transformation of the store under Shirinbai's stewardship was a testament to her resilience and adaptability. What had once been a place of spirits now served as a beacon of stability and support during uncertain times. The shelves, though filled with different goods, still held the same sense of familiarity and trust. The General Provisions Store was not just a business; it became a place of refuge, a symbol of Shirinbai's determination to provide for her family and serve the community, no matter the challenges that came their way. Just as the Nasik Hotel and the Bed and Breakfast had been before it, the General Provisions Store became a cornerstone of the community, where family, neighbors, and friends came together in the spirit of survival and solidarity.

The Surf Ladies of Nashik

In 1962, my grandmother, Silloo, was part of a pioneering team tasked with launching Surf in Nasik city. This team was handpicked for its strength and expertise, and their mission was no small feat. Surf was a new product in the Indian market, and the challenge wasn't just about introducing it, it was about changing the way people thought about washing and cleaning.

Along with Silloo, there were several other dedicated individuals who played key roles in this monumental task, including Sheroo Kolhapurwalla, Mehernosh Mistry's mother-in-law. Together, they formed a dynamic group, each contributing their skills to ensure the product's success.

Their daily routine was rigorous. Each morning, the team would gather at a designated spot, wearing crisp blue and white saris, colors that would soon become synonymous with Surf. They carried large metal buckets filled with water, packets of Surf powder, and a few well-used cloth pieces that had been intentionally stained with oil, mud, and turmeric. These stains, common in Indian households, were their biggest challenge, and their greatest selling point.

Sheroo Kolhapurwalla and Silloo Mistry's role was particularly demanding. Armed with their buckets, they would go door-to-door, visiting house after house, knocking on wooden doors and calling out to housewives. Convincing these women to switch from traditional bar soaps to a powder detergent was not easy. Many were skeptical, after all, how could a powder clean better than the trusted blue bars they had been using for years?

The demonstrations were the heart of their strategy. One member of the team would fill a bucket with water, while another would stir in a measured scoop of Surf powder, ensuring it dissolved properly. Then, in full view of the skeptical housewives, they would take a heavily soiled cloth, dunk it into the bucket, and swish it around. As they worked the fabric, the foam would rise, a visible sign of Surf's power. Within minutes, they would pull out the cloth, wring it, and hold it up against the sunlight, the stains would have significantly faded, if not vanished completely.

Some housewives were still unconvinced. That's when another team member would challenge them: "Try it yourself!" A hesitant woman would step forward, rubbing a bit of Surf between her fingers, feeling its texture, before nervously scrubbing a dirty patch of her own saree. Within moments, as the fabric brightened, her doubt would turn into delight.

To reinforce their message, Silloo and Sheroo also explained the science behind the product in simple terms. They spoke about how Surf's formula created powerful foam that lifted dirt particles instead of grinding them deeper into the cloth, like bar soaps often did. "This means your clothes last longer," they would add, appealing to the frugal nature of homemakers.

Some members of the team were responsible for logistics. They would replenish the water in buckets, distribute free sample sachets, and take note of interested customers who wanted to buy a full packet. Others kept a keen eye on the surroundings, ensuring the demonstration area stayed clean and organized, as first impressions mattered greatly.

—

By the time they moved to the next house, their hands were wrinkled from constant contact with soapy water, their sarees damp at the edges, and their voices slightly hoarse from hours of talking, but their spirits remained high. Every converted customer was a small victory, and collectively, these small victories-built Surf into a trusted household name.

The efforts of these women were not just about selling a product; they were about transforming habits, reshaping traditions, and empowering homemakers with better choices. Thanks to their dedication, Surf became a staple in Indian households, and its legacy continues even today.

The team's efforts were instrumental in Surf's success, and their collective commitment to the task laid the groundwork for a product that would go on to become a household name across the country.

Boys Town School Canteen
There was a time when my grandparents, Jamshed and Silloo, received a contract with a local school called Boys Town, where they took on the responsibility of providing home-cooked meals to the students in their canteen. This venture became more than just a business for them; it was a side hustle that allowed them to serve the community with care and dedication. While Jamshed and Silloo managed the canteen, it was Jamshed's brother and sister, Minoo and Manek, who took care of the store.

Minoo and Manek handled the day-to-day operations, while Silloo would wake up early every morning, preparing fresh, nutritious meals with love and attention to detail. Jamshed, meanwhile, would hop onto his cycle and deliver the food to the canteen, ensuring everything arrived on time and piping hot. The canteen quickly became a beloved spot for the students, and over the years, many people grew up eating the delicious food that Silloo lovingly prepared. It was a simple yet profound service, one that brought joy and nourishment to countless children, and I can proudly say that for many of them, the taste of home-cooked meals from Boys Town School Canteen will forever be associated with my grandmother's cooking.

Revival of the Store
When the prohibition was lifted in 1966, S.B. Mistry & Sons reopened its doors. The return was met with great enthusiasm from the community, and the store quickly regained its status as a household name. The family business became synonymous with trust, quality, and tradition. The store thrived under the watchful eyes of successive generations, each contributing their unique strengths to the business. From Shirinbai's unwavering determination to her children Minoo, Manek and Jamshed's innovations, the legacy of Jamsetjee Nowrojee & Co. lives on in S.B. Mistry & Sons.

Fun Fact: When the prohibition ended and our shop reopened in 1966, the atmosphere was nothing short of electrifying. Massive crowds gathered outside, cheering and celebrating as our family enthusiastically attended to customers, handing out bottles of liquor with smiles and laughter. But the real reason behind the crowd wasn't just the reopening, it was the presence of Bollywood's heartthrob, Dharmendra, casually seated on a bench outside!

His effortless charm and magnetic presence turned our humble relaunch into an unforgettable spectacle. Fans flocked not only to catch a glimpse of him but also to be part of what felt like a once-in-a-lifetime event. For months afterward, while shooting a film nearby, Dharmendra became a regular visitor, often stopping by for a chat and a drink, bringing a sparkle of Bollywood glamour to our little shop.

To this day, we treasure that very bench, now a cherished piece of our family's history, a reminder of when a legend's presence elevated our story to something truly extraordinary. It's not every day a small family business gets its own brush with stardom, and we take great pride in saying our store's revival was blessed by none other than Dharmendra himself

The 2017 Setback
The business faced another significant setback in 2017, during the tenure of my father, Darayus Mistry, who was then leading the firm. By this time, the ancestors who had established and nurtured the business were no longer with us. My father had taken up the mantle, continuing the legacy of his forebears with the same dedication and determination. In 2017, the government passed a law banning liquor stores located within 500 meters of a highway. This decision, while aimed at curbing road accidents, brought unintended consequences for businesses like ours. S.B. Mistry & Sons, located near a major road, was forced to shut down temporarily.

At that time, we feared history was repeating itself. We thought the business might suffer the same fate as it had during the prohibition era--shut down under government restrictions. It felt like the same helplessness that Shirinbai had once faced in a time of adversity.

For months, the store remained closed as the family explored legal avenues and awaited the government's revision of the law. It was a trying period, full of uncertainty, and we feared that our loyal customers would be lost.

Finally, when the ban was partially lifted, the store reopened its doors to the relief of the family and its loyal customers. The reopening of the shop was a sight worth seeing. Customers, many of whom had been waiting anxiously for months, would enter the store bowing down or even touching the ground, as though entering a temple, to mark their respect and gratitude that the shop had finally reopened. It was a truly humbling moment, seeing how much trust the community had placed in the business. The expressions on their faces spoke volumes, and the air was thick with emotions.

Even more touching were the emotional customers who came in and shared their joy. They spoke of how the shop had been a part of their lives for generations, how they had come to this very place with their grandparents, then their parents, and now with their own children. The shop, they said, was the only constant thing in the city that had remained through the changing times.
For them, it was not just a place of business, but a piece of history, a symbol of continuity and tradition in a world that had seen so much change. Their words filled us with pride and reaffirmed the deep connection we had with our community. The resilience demonstrated by my father during this time is something I will always admire. He ensured that the business bounced back stronger, maintaining the trust of its patrons and continuing the legacy.

The COVID-19 Pandemic

Just as the store had finally recovered from the 2017 setback, fate presented yet another formidable challenge in the form of the COVID-19 pandemic. Like countless other businesses, S.B. Mistry & Sons was forced to close its doors during the lockdowns, plunging the family into yet another period of uncertainty. The pandemic was unlike anything the world had seen before, and it tested not only the resilience of the business but also the very core of my father's leadership. Navigating this unprecedented crisis, my father was confronted with decisions that no one could have predicted.

In the face of such adversity, my father's optimism never wavered. While others scrambled to survive, he saw the pandemic as an opportunity to reevaluate and reshape the future of the business.
He took the time to restructure, to innovate, and to ensure that S.B. Mistry & Sons would not just survive the pandemic but emerge stronger, better equipped to thrive in a post-pandemic world. His vision and unwavering dedication to the family legacy steered the company through the storm, proving that even in the darkest times, hope and determination could lead the way.

A Legacy of Leadership

Throughout these present-day challenges, my father has been the backbone of the business. His ability to lead with both courage and compassion has kept the family legacy alive. The upkeep of the house, the seamless functioning of the store, and the preservation of the family's rich history are all testaments to his dedication. The family home, often referred to as a "white elephant," requires constant care and attention.

Over the years, it has become increasingly difficult to manage its upkeep, but my father has done so with remarkable grace and diligence. The story of the Mistry family is not just a chronicle of a business, it is the story of a family that has weathered storms, adapted to change, and stood the test of time. To this day, the Mistry family stands as a reminder of what can be achieved when a family unites to face life's challenges head-on. It is more than just a business or home; it is a legacy, a way of life, and a tribute to the generations who built it from the ground up.

The next time you walk through the doors of our house and store-S.B. Mistry & Sons, remember that it is not just a store, it is a living piece of history, a symbol of endurance, and a testament to the Mistry family's indomitable spirit.

Chapter 3: Silloo and Jamshed: The Foundations We Stand On

I wish I could say that I remember my grandparents, Silloo and Jamshed, vividly. But the truth is, I was too young when they passed away, and my memories of them are more like faded photographs in an old album, beautiful, treasured, but incomplete. What I know of them has been pieced together through stories, anecdotes, and the way my family speaks of them with unwavering reverence. The only image I carry of them is from the timeless portraits that grace the walls of our hall, standing as silent sentinels of memory and legacy.

Silloo, whom I fondly called Baapi, was the matriarch of the family, but not in the traditional, gentle sense often romanticized. She was strict, sharp, and commanded respect in every room she entered. People were often scared to be around her, and this included her three daughter-in-law's, Rati, Mahrukh and Hutoxi who were terrified of her strict demeanor. Yet, they all knew she loved them deeply. Her love wasn't expressed through soft words or hugs; it was in her actions, her unyielding discipline, and her insistence on the best for her family. She was straightforward and always to the point, never sugarcoating her words. I've heard tales of her running the household with an iron will. Whether it was ensuring the kitchen was spotless or that family traditions were upheld to the letter, Baapi's standards were unwavering. Her strictness, however, was balanced by her ability to care deeply. Beneath her stern exterior lay a woman whose actions spoke louder than her words, someone who believed in tough love because she knew it would keep the family strong and united.

The reason behind my craziness and love for the British Royal Family stems from our dear Silloo. That bug of loving royalty started from her, I guess I inherited it from her. Now don't ask me why or how, just know that both grandmother and grandson have this in common. Silloo was the Queen of Gool Mahal. I am just going to leave this out there as a secret between grandson and grandmother.

It is often said by my aunts, uncles, and cousins that if Baapi were alive today and found out that I had been admitted to a boarding school, she would have raised an absolute storm. She was the kind of lady who wouldn't have let such a decision slide without making her opinions known loud and clear. The whole house would have been turned upside down, her voice echoing through the walls as she demanded an explanation.

Every family member, from the youngest to the oldest, would have been summoned, where her sharp gaze would have left everyone too nervous to speak. She would have fought tooth and nail to bring me back home, insisting that no grandchild of hers would stay away from home. Even the mere thought of her reaction makes us laugh now, imagining her pacing the halls, hands on her hips, her words cutting through the air like a whip. That was the force of her personality, unwavering, fierce, and unapologetically protective of her family.

Jamshed, or Bawa as I called him, was the complete opposite of Baapi. He was soft-spoken, shy, and reserved, a man whose quiet strength brought a sense of calm to the family. Unlike Silloo's commanding presence, Jamshed preferred to stay in the background, letting his actions and gentle words do the talking. He was a man of few words, but when he spoke, his words carried wisdom and kindness.

While Silloo ruled the household with discipline, Jamshed provided balance with his quiet, nurturing nature. He was the kind of person who could make you feel at ease with just a look or a soft pat on the back. I've been told he was a great listener, someone who would patiently hear out everyone's worries and provide thoughtful advice.

I've always envied my siblings for the time they had with our grandparents. Benaifer, Yasmin, Sanaya, and Del-ara have stories of moments spent at their feet, learning, laughing, and feeling loved. I've heard about how Bawa would lift them up in his strong arms or how Baapi would sneak them an extra helping of dessert when no one was looking or the tales of Baapi's stern looks that could silence a room and Bawa's quiet chuckles that could instantly warm your heart. These stories have become a part of my memory too, as if I had been there, watching it all unfold from the sidelines.

Though I don't have personal memories of them, their legacy is everywhere. It's in the way our family holds tight to the traditions they valued, in the stories we still tell about their contrasting personalities, and in the way we've inherited their values. Baapi's strictness taught us discipline, while Bawa's gentleness showed us the importance of kindness and understanding.

Even now, years after they have passed, whenever we all meet for dinner or a family function, their stories inevitably come up. Sitting around the table, we laugh about Baapi's strictness, share memories of her sharp but loving words, and reminisce about Bawa's gentle, quiet demeanor. As the youngest in the family, these moments feel incredibly special to me. I love listening to my siblings, and older relatives recount their memories of our ancestors.

There's something magical about hearing the way their lives influenced ours, even from a distance of time. For me, it's like peeking into a time I never got to experience but feel deeply connected to through these shared stories.

I often think about what they would say if they saw us now. Their grandchildren grown up, carrying forward the Mistry name. I'd like to believe they would be proud, not just of our achievements but of the way we've held on to the essence of what they stood for: kindness, love, and unity. So, while I may not have memories of holding their hands or sitting on their laps, I feel their presence every day. They are the invisible threads that bind us together, the quiet voices reminding us of where we came from and the responsibility we have to carry their legacy forward. Silloo and Jamshed may not have been a part of my childhood in the way I wish they were, but they are, without a doubt, a part of who I am.

Chapter 4: The Timeless Charm of Minoo and Manek

Let us talk about my Grand uncle and aunt, Minoo and Manek. Who I would fondly call Minoo Kaka and Fuiji.

Minoo Kaka wasn't just a granduncle to me; he was the grandfather I never had the chance to remember. He was a character larger than life, a blend of wit, mischief, and love that filled every corner of the house. My earliest and perhaps most cherished memory of him is from when I was five or six years old. I would climb onto his lap as he sat with his glass of whisky, and he'd pour a little soda for me in a separate glass so we could "cheers" together. Those moments felt like a private club, just the two of us, sharing a bond no one else could touch. To keep me entertained, he would take empty soda bottles and carefully balance them one on top of the other, his hands steady with the precision of a craftsman. Sometimes he would even juggle with the empty bottles, something he learnt from the German circus days. He loved his drink as much as he loved me, and those little rituals became a cornerstone of our relationship.

Minoo Kaka's daily routine was another testament to his unique personality. Every morning, he would set out walking to Bhadrakali Bazaar, a bustling local market in Nashik. The journey itself was an event. He'd pass by the homes of relatives along the way, stopping for a cup of tea or a snack at each house. He was immensely popular in the neighborhood, known for his hearty laugh and sharp wit.
By the time he reached the bazaar, he was like a local celebrity, greeted warmly by the vendors he'd known for years. Minoo Kaka was fiercely loyal to his chosen vegetable and fruit sellers. No amount of persuasion could make him switch vendors.

"I know their produce is the best," he would say, brushing off suggestions to explore other options. And the vendors adored him right back, they reserved their freshest produce for him, knowing he'd always come back. Week after week, year after year, he brought home the raw materials for our large joint family of 18 members, both hands laden with heavy bags full of vegetables and fruits. As he aged, the family began urging him to use a rickshaw instead of walking such long distances. But for the longest time, he resisted, saying, "Walking keeps me young." Only when his body could no longer handle the strain did he reluctantly agree.

Minoo Kaka's reputation extended beyond the bazaar. Salespeople from liquor companies often visited the shop, eager to have him taste and provide feedback on their newly launched whiskey or rum. True to his blunt nature, he'd take a sip and declare, "Panchat che," meaning that it is "not good" if it didn't meet his high standards. There was no sugarcoating with him, he was direct and to the point, and people respected that honesty.

During the days of the General Provisional Store, the shop wasn't just a hub for essentials; it was a stage where glamour met everyday life. The radiant Indian actress Begum Para, a star of her time, was a regular visitor. Her trips to buy eggs and bread turned mundane moments into something magical. Each time she stepped into the store, her grace and poise seemed to light up the space, and Minoo Kaka, usually the epitome of calm and control, would suddenly become a bundle of nerves and delight. He would fuss over her orders with extra care, his hands almost trembling as he handed her the neatly packed groceries.

———

The boys, little Pervez, Mehernosh, and Darayus, who were often busy wreaking havoc in and around the shop, were given stern warnings whenever she arrived. "Be on your best behavior, boys, she's here!" Minoo Kaka would say, his voice both commanding and pleading. For those few moments, the rowdy little trio would transform into picture-perfect gentlemen, creating an atmosphere of almost comedic reverence for the stunning star.

Then there was Mahendra Sandhu, the rugged action hero known for his daredevil roles, who once strolled into the shop, oozing confidence and charisma. Sandhu, clearly hoping to make an impression, kept casually dropping his own name into the conversation, perhaps expecting fanfare or at least a flicker of awe.

He leaned casually on the counter and said, "Main Mahendra Sandhu hoon. Action ka hero."

Minoo Kaka, busy arranging packets of sugar, didn't even look up.

"Haan, toh?" he replied, unimpressed.

Sandhu blinked, momentarily thrown off, then recovered. "Main aksar yahan aata hoon...."

"Haan haan, jo bhi ho, ab bolo kya chahiye?" Minoo Kaka cut him off, his tone so blunt it could've been one of Sandhu's action-dialogues.

"I uh... ek bread aur do eggs," Sandhu mumbled, his larger-than-life persona shrinking a bit.

The contrast between Sandhu's self-assured demeanor and Minoo Kaka's unruffled attitude was pure comedy gold.

—

It became an instant family classic, a tale we narrate even now with roaring laughter, remembering the time when the star-struck and the star both played their parts in the colorful history of our humble store.

As a child, I was utterly fascinated by Minoo Kaka and Fuiji's saggy, wrinkled skin. Their hands and cheeks seemed so soft and full of texture, almost magical to my little mind. I would sit beside them, touching their hands and cheeks over and over, marveling at the feel of their wrinkles. They would laugh indulgently, letting me explore, never shooing me away.

There was a playfulness about Minoo Kaka that made him unforgettable. I can still see him peering through my bedroom door, his face framed by the mesh, grinning as he asked, "What are you doing?" Sometimes he'd interrupt my tutoring sessions, shouting through the house, asking if I was done studying yet. Far from being annoying, these interruptions were like bursts of sunlight, breaking the monotony of my day and reminding me that life wasn't just about books and lessons. He had a knack for making the ordinary feel extraordinary.

One of my favorite memories is the time he pretended to be hypnotized by me and my sister, Del-ara. We were dangling something from the dining table, just goofing around, trying to see if Del-ara could hypnotize me, when he suddenly slumped his head down and went completely still. For a few terrifying moments, we thought we had accidentally hypnotized him.
My sister and I panicked, unsure of what to do, only to have him suddenly burst out laughing, his eyes twinkling with mischief. He had a way of turning even the smallest moments into adventures.

His sense of humor was legendary, and his sharp tongue often left people either laughing or speechless. My dad and uncles would often share stories of his quick wit. One of my favorites was about the time a customer rudely remarked, "Oh, you're still alive?" Without missing a beat, Minoo Kaka replied, "Yes, I'm waiting for you to die first." Then there were the tales of him dealing with difficult customers at the shop, one particularly vivid story involved someone flashing bright car lights in his face. Minoo Kaka, of course, didn't just take it quietly. He would end up using some amazing Parsi phrases which I cannot really mention in this book. But rest assured, he would give them a good shouting.

His responses were always clever, cutting, and unforgettable. It wasn't just his humor that made him special. He had a deeply caring side that showed in the most unexpected ways. My mom often made me study behind closed doors, determined that I focus on my lessons. Yet, there was Minoo Kaka, sneaking up to the door, tapping lightly, and whispering to her to let me out.
"Come on, just for a little while," he'd plead. "We'll watch Tom and Jerry together." My mom, exasperated but unable to resist his charm, would relent, and off we'd go to the living room, where we'd laugh together over the antics of a cartoon cat and mouse.

As he got older and found himself confined to a wheelchair, his fun-loving spirit remained intact. No matter his physical limitations, his mischievous glint never faded.

I would eagerly count down the days until my holidays from boarding school, knowing that Minoo Kaka would be waiting for me. He'd sit in his wheelchair at home, a big smile lighting up his face as soon as I walked through the door. In the evenings, as my family gathered around the dining table, I'd tell stories of my school life, the adventures, anecdotes, and everything in between. Even if it was past his bedtime, he would sit quietly, listening intently, soaking in every word.
He would often ask me with genuine curiosity, "Do you like your school? Did you make any girlfriends?" His teasing questions never failed to make me blush, and he'd chuckle at my shyness. Those moments were filled with warmth, a reminder that no matter how much time had passed or how far I had been, I was always his boy, and he was always there, waiting for me with that same unwavering affection.

Even when life threw challenges his way, he faced them with humor and resilience. After a fall, he went around singing the Parsi children's tune, "Mara papa ni che motor gadi," as if to remind us all to take life a little less seriously. Comparing his new wheelchair to a motor gari. His humor was his armor, his way of connecting with people and reminding them that even in the darkest times, there was always room for a smile. Minoo Kaka's presence in my life was a gift. He was the kind of person who could light up a room with his stories, his antics, and his laughter. For me, he wasn't just family, he was a source of joy, a wellspring of love, and a reminder that the best moments in life are often the simplest. Even today, when I think of him, I can't help but smile, grateful for the countless memories he gave me. He wasn't just a part of my childhood; he was its brightest, happiest corner.

Minoo Kaka filled my childhood with laughter and warmth, but my memories of Manek, whom I fondly called Fuiji, are just as vivid and cherished. Fuiji wasn't just my grand aunt; she was like a grandmother to me. I don't have many memories of my grandmother Silloo, as she passed away when I was too young to truly know her. Fuiji stepped into that role effortlessly, giving me the comfort, guidance, and love that only a grandmother can offer.

One of the strongest memories I have of Fuiji is tied to her scent, a signature that was unmistakably hers. She was always covered in Yardley powder, a luxury my aunts and uncles would bring back from their foreign trips. Every hug I gave her came with the comforting, powdery fragrance of Yardley. It was like being enveloped in a soft cloud of familiarity and love. Fuiji always wore gowns. Flowing, comfortable, and uniquely hers. On special occasions like Polly Kaka's birthday, she would wear a new gown, treating the day with an extra sense of celebration and importance. It was her way of marking the occasion with her own special flair.

Fuiji had a sharp tongue, and her bluntness was legendary. She had no filter just like her brother, especially when it came to guests. If someone had gained weight, she would announce it the moment they stepped in: "Oh, you've gone fat!" Or, if someone was still unmarried, she'd casually remark, "You haven't found anyone yet? Why not?" Her words often left people flustered, but her bluntness wasn't meant to hurt. It was simply her way, straightforward, unvarnished, and unapologetic.

She had a curious habit that could sometimes become a bit embarrassing. Whenever someone brought something new into the house be it clothing, utensils, or a new gadget, Fuiji would immediately ask where it was bought from and how much it cost. "How much did you pay for this?" she'd ask unabashedly, her voice filled with genuine curiosity. While her questions sometimes made the rest of us squirm, they were never ill-intentioned just a reflection of her natural inquisitiveness.

My favorite memories of her often involved her little acts of rebellion and mischief. She had a secret stash of chocolates and biscuits in her cupboard, and every now and then, she would sneak into my room to drop a treat on my desk. It felt like our little secret, a gesture that said, "I'm thinking of you."

Then there were the times when Mahrukh Kaki my aunt, would bring over some delicious food for the family. Fuiji, despite her health restrictions, couldn't resist sneaking into the kitchen for a taste. Whether it was spicy biryani, tangy curries, or anything forbidden, she'd find a way to sample it. Her late-night escapades were the stuff of family legends. She had an insatiable love for chocolates, pani puri, and anything sour or tangy. We'd wake up in the morning to find empty boxes in the kitchen, and we all knew it was Fuiji. The sight of those open, half-empty containers was a testament to her zest for life, even in the smallest pleasures.

One of the most touching stories about her comes not from my own memories but from the tales my parents and uncles have shared. When I was away at boarding school, I would write letters home, pouring my heart out onto paper. Fuiji eagerly awaited those letters.

She'd sit at the dining table, her chair becoming her throne of anticipation, and ask my father every day, "Has my little Baba sent a letter today?" That name, Baba, felt like a term of endearment that encapsulated all her love for me.

Fuiji was also a die-hard fan of Amitabh Bachchan. She would watch his movies with a level of devotion and excitement that was unmatched. Anytime his name was mentioned, her face would light up with joy. She would watch his movies over and over again, sometimes taking complete control of the remote, leaving me with no choice but to sit and watch alongside her.
If it was her chance to have the remote, I knew better than to argue. I remember one particular evening when "Sholay" was airing on TV, and I was hoping to watch Scooby Doo instead.
But Fuiji, with a mischievous smile and her sharp glare, firmly said, "Amitabh is more important than your silly dog show!" She handed me a plate of snacks and patted the seat next to her, so I had no escape. By the end of the movie, she was mouthing the dialogues and clapping enthusiastically during Amitabh's scenes, while I had no choice but to join in.

She even made me watch "Kaun Banega Crorepati" with her religiously, insisting that I sit quietly and answer the questions like a contestant. "Kerfegar, you'll win all the crores!" she would say with a grin. While I didn't always understand her fascination, seeing her so engrossed and happy made it all worth it. Her admiration for Amitabh Bachchan became another endearing part of her personality, adding to the many quirks that made her so unforgettable.

Today, I live in her room. I've redone it to match my own tastes, but I've kept its essence intact. The scent of Yardley powder, the warmth of her memories, and the echoes of her laughter still linger in the walls. It's a space that feels alive with her spirit, a constant reminder of the love and mischief she brought into our lives.

I still remember the nights I spent sleeping in this very room as a young kid. There were three beds in the room, one for Fuiji, one for Minoo Kaka, and one that I would quietly claim as my own. On one particular night, I had trouble falling asleep. I kept tossing and turning, trying to find comfort on the firm mattress. Sensing my restlessness, Fuiji called out softly, "Sui jaa, dikra, sui jaa… nahi toh bhoot aavi jase!" (Go to sleep, child, or the ghost will come!) I knew she was teasing me, but her voice had a playful menace that sent a chill down my spine. I immediately sat up, wide-eyed, and begged her to tell me there was no ghost. She burst out laughing, her signature giggle filling the room as she patted the bed beside her, asking me to come sleep next to her.

I remember how safe I felt curling up on her bed, the scent of her Yardley powder lingering in the air, and her hand gently resting on my back until I drifted off to sleep. The warmth of that moment has stayed with me. Even now, when I lie in this room, I can almost feel her presence, her teasing, her kindness, and her endless affection. It's moments like those that make this space feel alive, as if she's still here, watching over me.

I was in the 8th grade, preparing to leave for my boarding school, when I first experienced the profound sting of loss. The news of Minoo Kaka's passing hit me like a wave I wasn't ready to face.

It felt surreal, just a few days ago, I had been sharing stories with him and now, the house felt quieter, emptier, as if it had lost its heartbeat.

And then, within a few months, Fuiji too left us. Her passing was even harder for me to process. She had been my grandmother in every sense, filling the void left by my paternal grandmother, Silloo. Fuiji's blunt humor, her sneaky chocolates, and her infectious laughter, all of it vanished in an instant. It was the first time I had seen a dead body, and it terrified me. I called out to them, hoping they'd open their eyes, but they didn't. The realization that I would never hear their voices or see their smiles again was overwhelming.

Their deaths marked the end of a beautiful era of my childhood. No more cartoons with Minoo Kaka, no more secret treats from Fuiji, no more lighthearted pranks. For the first time in my life, I understood the weight of permanence, the finality of loss. The house felt heavier, quieter, as if mourning along with us.

Even now, I miss them deeply. I often think of them in good spirits, sitting together in heaven, sipping tea and chuckling at my antics. I imagine Minoo Kaka with his ever-ready smile and Fuiji with her Yardley-scented mischief, watching over me. Their absence is a reminder of how blessed I was to have them, and their memory continues to guide me, filling my heart with warmth and nostalgia.

Chapter 5: Builders of the Modern Legacy: Parvez, Mehernosh and Darayus

PARVEZ

Parvez Mistry, known to us all as Polly, holds a significant place in my heart. The eldest of the three brothers, born in 1950, and the first grandchild of Shirinbai, Polly Kaka is the embodiment of warmth, generosity, and a life well-lived. He is the first child of Silloo and Jamshed, and, as tradition holds, the "Prince" of the family as Manek aunty- Fuiji called him, the one who lit up the entire family with his energy and spirit. Growing up, Polly Kaka was not just an uncle to me but a friend, a mentor, and a guiding figure in countless ways.

He started his career working in a bank, a conventional choice for someone of his caliber, but it wasn't long before he ventured into the world of business, following in the footsteps of his grandmother, Shirinbai. Like her, he recognized the importance of serving the community, and so he opened his own general provisions store, KitKat. The store, much like Shirinbai's General Provisions Store, quickly became a beloved institution in the city. Polly Kaka's KitKat store was known for its exceptional chocolates, buttery popcorn, and a selection of other delightful treats that drew people from all corners of the city.The store had an aura of charm and character, with shelves stocked with a variety of sweet and savory snacks, making it the go-to place for those craving something special. Its reputation for quality spread far and wide, and it wasn't long before KitKat became a local favorite, just as Shirinbai's store had been many years before.

Through KitKat, Polly Kaka continued the family's legacy of providing not just goods, but a place where the community could gather, connect, and share in simple pleasures.

One of my earliest memories of KitKat was spending afternoons there, sitting atop stacked packets of popcorn, sipping on warm Bournvita milk. While I relished the sweet drink, my older sisters, Benaifer and Yasmin, kept a watchful eye on me.
I remember Benaifer engrossed in reading the first Harry Potter book while Yasmin sat nearby, listening to music on her Walkman. The store was a hive of activity, buzzing with customers and the aroma of snacks and sweets. Even then, I felt a sense of pride seeing how much people admired and appreciated what Polly Kaka had built. Later, Polly Kaka expanded into the lottery business, a venture that, like his previous ones, reflected his tendency to dive into diverse fields with enthusiasm and commitment.

Food has always been a central theme in the bond I share with Polly Kaka and his wife Rati Kaki. Together, the three of us have spent countless moments indulging in all sorts of culinary delights. From rich and creamy sweets to decadent chocolates, from fluffy donuts to steaming cups of coffee, we relish every bite and sip with unspoken camaraderie. Polly Kaka's love for good food is infectious, and Rati Kaki complements it perfectly with her extraordinary cooking skills. These shared moments around food have become cherished rituals, adding flavor, literally and figuratively, to our lives. It's no wonder that Polly Kaka, with his entrepreneurial flair, once owned an ice cream parlour. This endeavor was more than just a business; it was a reflection of his passion for creating joy through simple pleasures, like a scoop of cold, creamy goodness on a warm day.

But it's not just about sweets and snacks. Polly Kaka's margaritas deserve a chapter of their own. On special occasions, he crafts these magical drinks that are nothing short of an art form. With just the right balance of tangy lime, a hint of sweetness, and that icy cold punch, his margaritas are a masterpiece. I can still picture the way he prepares them with precision and flair, pouring the frosty mix into salt-rimmed glasses while sharing stories of his younger days. These moments, sipping on his signature margaritas, often accompanied by laughter and heartfelt conversations, are among the most treasured memories of my life. There's something deeply comforting about the way Polly Kaka's margaritas bring people together, fostering a sense of joy and togetherness that only he can create.

But, for all his ventures, the most important and life-defining one was his partnership with my aunt, Rati, whom I lovingly call Rati Kaki. Polly Kaka and Rati kaki's relationship is a love story in its purest form. Married in 1975, their union was a love match, a testament to the power of true affection. Rati Kaki, the first daughter-in-law of Silloo and Jamshed, was an absolute blessing to our family. She became the epitome of grace and strength, supporting Polly Kaka through thick and thin. Rati Kaki became my partner in crime, my secret weapon.
Whenever I needed something, or wanted to get away with something, I always knew I could count on her. She has always been a constant in my life, a dependable source of love and understanding. One of the many things I will forever be grateful for is her culinary talent. Her exquisite egg making skills are legendary, perfectly cooked, mouth-watering, and delicious. No one in the family can ever replicate her double fried eggs, and they have become somewhat of a family tradition.

Polly and Rati's union also brought two daughters into the world, Benaifer and Yasmin. As the firstborn, they became the Elizabeth and Margaret of the family as I like to secretly call them. We will talk about these two legendary sisters in the coming few chapters. They carry with them the legacy of their parents, a legacy that is filled with love, laughter, and the undying bond of family.

My earliest memories of Polly Kaka go back to when I was just a toddler, around five or six years old. He would take me on Sunday morning drives, a tradition that became deeply ingrained in my life. I remember sitting next to him in the passenger seat, fiddling with the seatbelt and the car's music system, watching the world pass by. These drives were never rushed, and by the time we were heading back, I would have usually dozed off in the comfort of the car, feeling safe and protected.

Even now, as I look back, I remember the peace and warmth of those moments. Polly Kaka and Rati Kaki still carry on their tradition of long drives, albeit less frequently. They always make sure to include me, and I cherish these coffee stops that often accompany these trips. The conversations we have, about new technology, how to use a specific feature on the phone, life at my boarding school, or even stories about the house, have become some of my most cherished memories. Whether discussing my dad and Mehernosh uncles' antics or reminiscing about a time when a thief had broken into the house, these moments of shared time are precious.

During my 10th standard board exams, when my mother was being strict about my studies and wouldn't allow me to go out much, Polly Kaka and Rati Kaki were there to offer me small moments of joy.

———

They would surprise me with cappuccinos from Cafe Coffee Day, my favorite, a simple yet thoughtful gesture that provided me with much-needed comfort during those stressful days. Even though they might have seemed like small moments at the time, they have stayed with me for years.

What people often say about Polly Kaka and me is that we share an uncanny resemblance, not just in appearance but in our mannerisms and quirks. For instance, we both have a particular way of eating our food, we insist on having fruits neatly cut and placed in a bowl, rather than eating them off directly. The same goes for cake; we prefer it on a proper plate, not off a tissue paper! We are often teased for being so alike. We share an aversion to the smell of aachar and ghee, and people often joke that we are a carbon copy of each other, right down to our haircuts and antics. It's a comparison I take with great affection, as it reflects the bond Polly Kaka, and I share.

One of the things that defines Polly Kaka is his love for music. He is renowned for his vast collection of music cassettes, CDs, and LPs. Music has been a constant in his life, and it's something he has passed down to the next generation. Whether it's playing his favorite songs or sharing stories about how music has been a part of his life, Polly Kaka's passion for music has always been something I admire deeply. He would often regale me with stories of the house's early days, how bats and birds once flew inside the house through the open passage in the middle, or how Minoo Kaka would lock himself in a room along with a rat and not come out until he had killed the rat. Though these stories sent chills down my spine, they also gave me a glimpse into a world that was far more adventurous than I could have imagined.

There were other stories too, stories of the three
brothers dancing in the attic with their friends who
were apparently girls while Fuiji, the ever-vigilant
aunt, would come to check on them causing major
embarrassment for the brothers. Or how the
brothers would secretly sneak out at night with their
respective wives to avoid being scolded by their
mother for going on late night drives or ice-cream
breaks.

These stories of mischief and camaraderie are woven
into the fabric of our family, and Polly Kaka has
always been the one to share them with me.
One of my favorite stories involves the outhouse,
which Polly Kaka transformed into his personal
retreat, fondly called "Polly's Cottage." It became a
hub for music, relaxation, and camaraderie, where
neighbors would gather to study, party, or simply
enjoy good music. Though the outhouse eventually
fell into disrepair, its memory remains a testament
to Polly Kaka's creativity and love for bringing people
together.

In addition to Polly Kaka, Rati Kaki is a central figure
in my life, and together, they have created a home
filled with love, laughter, and memories. Rati Kaki,
with her gentle spirit and infectious laughter, has
always been my go-to person for advice, comfort,
and support. She has the ability to make everyone
feel at home, and her cooking especially her famous
eggs, is a source of comfort for everyone who has
had the privilege of tasting her food.

Rati Kaki and Polly Kaka are not just my family; they
are my role models. Their relationship, their love for
music, and their unwavering support for one another
have shaped my understanding of what true
partnership and love are. They have given me
countless memories to cherish and have helped mold
me into the person I am today.

—

Polly Kaka continues to be a living legend in our family, a figure whose influence is felt in everything we do. His love for music, his entrepreneurial spirit, and his unshakable bond with Rati Kaki are the pillars that have held me together through thick and thin. He is a constant source of wisdom, laughter, and love, and I am grateful for every moment spent with him. Together, Polly and Rati have made our family richer, not just in material wealth, but in love, warmth, and memories that will last a lifetime.

MEHERNOSH

Mehernosh Mistry, the middle child of the Mistry family, holds a special place in my heart. Born in 1951, he is known for his mischievous nature and fun-loving personality. I lovingly call him Mehernosh Kaka. Manek, his aunt, would often regale me with stories about his antics, painting a vivid picture of a young man who was always up to something playful but endearing. She would say that despite his mischief, he was deeply responsible when it came to certain things, like driving the family around or playing carefully with his niece. Both his parents and aunts trusted him implicitly, feeling completely safe when he was behind the wheel. I still remember her words: "When you grow up, learn to drive like Mehernosh, safe and bindass."

Fuiji also shared stories of how young Mehernosh would accompany his father, Jamshed, to auctions happening in and around the city. These outings were a special bonding time for father and son, who would spend hours together scouring the auctions for items to furnish the home. It was in these moments that Mehernosh Kaka developed a keen eye for quality and value, a trait that would later serve him well in his entrepreneurial endeavors.

His mischief, however, wasn't confined to family outings. Another tale that Fuiji often shared was how, as dusk fell, Mehernosh Kaka would shout random names or make strange noises from the window of the bungalow to scare unsuspecting passersby. His impish laughter would echo through the house as people tried to figure out where the eerie sounds were coming from.

One of the most infamous stories about Mehernosh Kaka's mischief involves a late-night visit to the Inayat Café in Nashik.

He and his two brothers, along with their friends, had gone there for a bite. As two of their friends, Viraf and Farokh, went inside to place an order, Mehernosh Kaka sitting in the driver's seat with the rest of the group, spotted two men relieving themselves on the street. Ever the prankster, he decided to flash the car's headlights on them. This angered the men, who immediately started approaching the car, ready for a confrontation. Thinking quickly, Mehernosh Kaka shouted for Farokh, one of the friends still inside the café. Hearing a Muslim name, the men assumed the group was "their own" and decided to back off. It's a story that still makes me chuckle every time I hear it.

A lesser-known chapter of his life, which has always intrigued me, is the time when he and Polly Kaka dabbled in selling roller belts. I imagine the two young and dashing brothers going around the city, charming customers with their wit and enthusiasm. While this venture may not have lasted, it spoke volumes about their entrepreneurial spirit, a trait that defined Mehernosh Kaka's later achievements.

In 1973, Mehernosh Kaka decided to take the Mistry name to even greater heights, following in the footsteps of his grandfather Banaji. With a vision of success and a deep sense of legacy, he opened his very own liquor store, Mistry Liquor Mart. The journey was not an easy one. It was born out of relentless hard work, countless long hours, and unwavering dedication. Alongside him every step of the way was Mahrukh Kaki, his partner in both life and business. Together, they poured their heart and soul into building Mistry Liquor Mart, ensuring it would stand as a testament to their perseverance.

—

Their efforts quickly bore fruit, and Mistry Liquor Mart soon became one of the most trusted and respected names in the city. The store was not just a business; it was an embodiment of the Mistry family's legacy of resilience, hard work, and a commitment to excellence.

Mehernosh Kaka married Mahrukh Kaki in 1985, and their union was nothing short of beautiful. I've always admired their relationship, which seemed to be built on mutual respect and unwavering support for each other. Together, they raised a wonderful daughter, Sanaya, my third sister. I'll delve more into her story later, but suffice it to say, she inherited the best qualities of both her parents.

As the business grew and demanded more of their time, Mehernosh Kaka and Mahrukh Kaki made the difficult decision to move closer to Mistry Liquor Mart, which was located in Nashik Road. Though the physical distance between their new home and the family's ancestral house was not enormous, it did mean fewer spontaneous visits and shared meals. As a child, I missed having them around as often, but as I've grown older, I've come to treasure the time I did get to spend with them even more. Their stories of the "good old days" are nothing short of fascinating, and each moment spent in their company is a gift.

One of the traditions that I hold closest to my heart is celebrating my birthday with the entire family. Over the years, it has become a custom for all three brothers and their families to gather on my special day. I insist on this celebration every year, as it fills me with immense joy to have everyone under one roof. This tradition is more than just a party; it is a celebration of love, unity, and the unbreakable bond we share as a family.

I feel deeply connected to my roots during these moments, surrounded by those who matter most to me. As we sit together, reminiscing about the golden days, sharing heartfelt stories, and basking in the warmth of familial love, I am overwhelmed with gratitude. These gatherings are a poignant reminder of how truly blessed I am to have such a loving and close-knit family.

One thing Mehernosh Kaka and I share is our extremely sensitive noses. Both of us are highly allergic to everything from dust to pollen. Whether it's sneezing fits, watery eyes, or the occasional cold, our noses seem to pick up on every irritant imaginable. It's a shared struggle that often becomes a source of lighthearted banter between us, adding another layer to the unique bond we share.

One of my earliest and fondest memories of them is from the time they invited us to a small party at their new villa. I was just a small kid, filled with excitement and curiosity. Everything about the house seemed grand and magical to me, and I couldn't resist exploring every corner. I distinctly remember sitting at the dining table next to little Sanaya, with my parents seated across from us. The table was laden with food, and I couldn't help but dive right in. Sodas, samosas, potato chips, everything was a treat for my young eyes and eager taste buds.

My enthusiasm didn't go unnoticed, as my parents shot me disapproving looks, silently urging me to behave. But in that moment, I was too lost in the joy of the feast to care. I had Sanaya sitting right beside me and Kaki on the other side, nothing could stop me from enjoying those sodas and samosas. Not even those disapproving looks from Mom and Dad.

—

Another cherished memory is from a day I spent with them before leaving for boarding school. It was a day filled with fun, laughter, and unforgettable moments. Mehernosh Kaka drove Sanaya, Delara, and me to a small play area, where we enjoyed dashing cars, rode the Ferris wheel, and bought balloons and toys. Kaka even bought me a toy boat, while my sisters treated me to chocolates.

The day didn't end there. Back at their house, we stayed up late watching movies, and Mahrukh Kaki amazed us all by creating a miniature volcano that erupted with "lava." The sheer excitement and wonder I felt watching that volcano are memories I hold close to my heart. The day culminated in a mouthwatering meal, which included my first taste of Mahrukh Kaki's legendary rum cake. Ah, the rum cake! Words cannot do justice to the sheer delight of that cake. It was a symphony of flavors, each bite a heavenly experience. To this day, it remains my favorite dessert.
During my time in boarding school, I would eagerly wait for visits from my parents, knowing they would bring me a slice of that magical cake. One such occasion led to a funny incident. After sneaking a piece of rum cake back to my dormitory, a friend commented that I smelled like alcohol, and he knew I was hiding a piece of that cake in my pocket. Panicking, I quickly handed him a packet of Maggi noodles that my parents had smuggled for me to buy his silence. Thankfully, the situation was resolved without any further trouble, and my secret indulgence remained just that, a secret.

Mahrukh Kaki and Mehernosh Kaka were also instrumental in helping me acquire my first digital camera. If you know me, you're aware of my intense fear of dogs. I can't go near them without feeling utterly petrified.

During one of our visits to their home, my father dared me to pet their dog, Snoopy, promising me a digital camera if I did. I was adamant about refusing until Mahrukh Kaki whispered to me, "Accept the challenge. I have a secret, and you'll get your camera. I promise." Reluctantly, I agreed, and she sprang into action. She brought out a muzzle for Snoopy, ensuring he couldn't bite, and with trembling hands, I managed to pet him. True to her word, I got my first digital camera, a cherished possession made all the more special by the story behind it.

Another dimension of my bond with Mahrukh Kaki is our shared love for reading and writing. In fact, when Mehernosh Kaka was courting her, he once wrote her a love letter. Being a teacher of literature and science, Mahrukh Kaki couldn't resist correcting the grammatical mistakes in the letter. Needless to say, that marked the end of his letter-writing days! Despite this, their love story continued to flourish, built on mutual respect and a shared sense of humor. To this day, this story gives me the giggles.

Beyond the fond memories and fun anecdotes, Mahrukh Kaki and Mehernosh Kaka have played an invaluable role in my upbringing. They are also the ones who have kept my dream of visiting the UK alive. A die-hard fan of Britain and the Royal Family, I often imagine myself visiting old palaces, enjoying tea in the gardens, exploring historic museums, marveling at Buckingham Palace, indulging in regal and grand dinners, staying at Ritz hotels and The Grantley Hall, and even experiencing a ride in a Rolls-Royce.

One of the most cherished and amusing aspects of my bond with Mahrukh Kaki is our ongoing joke about finding me a British bride. Over the years, this playful banter has become a delightful tradition whenever we discuss my dream of settling in the UK. Kaki teases me, saying that once I find the perfect British bride, everything else will fall into place. She even jokes about how we will be hosting a grand wedding at a historic English manor, complete with all the pomp and splendor of royal tradition. I can't help but laugh when she describes how she'll take charge of vetting potential matches, ensuring they have the poise and elegance to match my imagined British lifestyle.

Her playful encouragement adds a sense of lightheartedness to my aspirations while reminding me that I am surrounded by people who believe in my dreams and want to see me thrive.

Even though there was physical distance between us, my bond with Mehernosh Kaka and Mahrukh Kaki never wavered. Their home was a haven of love and warmth, a place where I always felt welcome. I cherish the memories of those moments, whether they were spent enjoying a delicious meal, sharing stories from the past, or simply sitting together and talking about life.

Mahrukh Kaki's sister, Rashna aunty, truly deserves a heartfelt mention. She has always been a beacon of kindness and warmth, making everyone feel welcome with her gentle nature and ever-sweet demeanor. As a young child of about seven or eight, I was utterly convinced that she was the mastermind behind the "Rasna" soft drink, purely because of her name.

In my innocent confidence, I would proudly declare to anyone who'd listen, "Rashna aunty makes Rasna! She owns the whole company! Yes, the whole company! She is my aunty! She is a multi-millionaire!"

It wasn't until I grew older that I realized the amusing truth, and to this day, we share a good laugh about my childhood misconception.

Back then, I even gave her a playful nickname, Sarbat aunty, our very own sweet Rasna! Her good-natured chuckles at my antics made those moments even more special. Beyond those fond memories, Rashna aunty holds a unique place in my heart as my unofficial "buffet buddy." Whenever our family dines out, the two of us invariably gravitate toward the buffet, eager to explore and sample every new dish on display. It's become our little tradition, one that adds an extra layer of joy to family outings.

Kaka and Kaki's dedication to their work, their unwavering support for each other, and their love for their family have always been a source of inspiration for me. They taught me the value of hard work, the importance of staying connected to one's roots, and the joy of sharing life's moments with loved ones. Alongside them, Rashna Aunty and Sanaya have been a shining example of these same values.

Together, Mehernosh Kaka, Mahrukh Kaki, Rashna aunty and Sanaya have shown me what it means to live a life rooted in love, laughter, and togetherness. Their stories, their wisdom, and the unwavering care they've shown me over the years have shaped me in countless ways. I adore them deeply and feel incredibly grateful for the beautiful bond we share.

Every memory with them is a treasure, and every moment spent in their company is a reminder of the strength and beauty of our family's legacy. Truly, they are the heart and soul of so many cherished moments in my life, and I feel blessed to have them as a part of my story.

DARAYUS

Darayus Mistry, my father, is the youngest child of Silloo and Jamshed Mistry, born in 1958. He grew up with a unique mix of pampered affection and mischievous energy that made him the charming, lively personality he is today. Dad has always been a story worth telling. His early days in Mumbai, where he pursued a career in interior design, were marked by ambition and hard work. He worked with some of the most prominent people in the field, collaborating with big names in the world of painting and design. The stories of his college days are peppered with tales of camaraderie, creativity, and hard-earned success, with his friends going on to become well-known figures in their respective fields.

However, Mumbai was only a chapter in his life, albeit a formative one. At around 24, the same age I am as I started to write this, he made a decision that would shape the rest of his life. He returned to Nashik to take on the responsibility of the family's ancestral business. The decision was monumental, not just for him but for the entire family. By taking over the business, Dad allowed his parents, uncle, and aunt to step back from their duties and enjoy the retirement they had earned through years of hard work. It wasn't just about managing a business; it was about upholding a legacy. He took over every aspect of the operations, ensuring the family's values and traditions were maintained while steering the business toward growth and success.

Dad also took on the monumental responsibility of maintaining our ancestral home. This grand house, lovingly built by generations before us, is a true white elephant. As each year passes, its upkeep becomes more and more challenging.

But Dad has taken care of it with a kind of devotion that only he is capable of. From repairs to renovations, from ensuring the plumbing works during monsoons to keeping its vintage charm alive, Dad has been the pillar that holds this house together. I often marvel at his dedication, thinking to myself, "I don't think I can ever do justice to how he has taken care of this house." It's not just a building; it's a living, breathing entity that thrives because of Dad's love and hard work.

Watching him manage the business while also taking care of the family instilled in me a deep respect for the value of hard work and selflessness. He truly became the backbone of our family, ensuring that both the business and the household were in good hands. In time, Dad married my mother, Hutoxi Mistry, the youngest daughter-in-law of the Mistry family and, as he often jokes, the final member of the "gang." Their marriage, unlike those of his elder brothers, was arranged. Yet, despite this, their bond has grown into a beautiful partnership rooted in love, understanding, and mutual respect.

They soon became parents to my sister, Delara, their firstborn, and five years later, they had me, Kerfegar. Mom was welcomed into the family with open arms, and she quickly adapted to life in a joint household. It wasn't easy for her, she had never lived in such an environment before, but she embraced her new life with grace and determination. Slowly, she took over the household responsibilities, allowing my grandmother, Silloo, to enjoy a well-deserved retirement.

My mother, in many ways, became the heart of our home. She's a woman of quiet strength, and her love for her family is evident in everything she does. Her actions have always spoken louder than words.

—

One of the most important lessons Delara, my sister, and I have learned from her is the importance of being there for your people. Whether it's sending food to someone during tough times or personally caring for someone in need, Mom has always shown us what it means to be kind. Her helping nature is reflected in her love for cooking, a talent she uses to bring joy and comfort to others. The meals she prepares aren't just food; they're expressions of her love and care. Watching her has taught us the value of kindness, not as an abstract concept but as something you demonstrate through your actions every single day.

Mom is also the most resourceful person I know. I remember countless occasions when friends, neighbors, or even acquaintances would approach her for help, and she would step in without hesitation. Her kitchen became a lifeline for many, especially during tough times. Whether it was sending warm meals to someone who was sick or organizing feasts for our family gatherings, she did it all with love and dedication. Her selflessness wasn't just about the big gestures but also the small, thoughtful acts that made people feel cared for. These actions left a deep impression on me and Delara, teaching us that being there for others is not just a duty but a privilege.

Dad, on the other hand, has always been our biggest cheerleader. One of the most profound lessons he has imparted to us is the importance of following our hearts. He has never pressured us into anything, always encouraging us to pursue our passions and dreams. Whether it was choosing a career, pursuing a hobby, or making life decisions, Dad's advice has always been simple: do what makes you happy. This freedom has been a gift, allowing Delara and me to explore our paths with confidence, knowing we have his unwavering support.

—

Their marriage is a testament to what a partnership should be. While Mom took charge of the household, Dad ensured the business flourished. Together, they built a life that balanced responsibility and joy.
My father's playful side, of course, hasn't dimmed with age. One of his longest-running jokes is the tale of "Lolita," his fictional girlfriend. He would regale us with stories of her charm and beauty, much to the annoyance of my mom and the amusement of Delara and me. Even though we all knew Lolita was a figment of his imagination, it never failed to make us laugh. It's this blend of humor and warmth that makes Dad so special. He has a way of making life lighter, even during the toughest times.

Mom, too, has her own brand of humor and discipline. During my 10th board exams, she took her role as a disciplinarian to a whole new level, insisting that I dedicate myself to studying. Coming from a school that prioritized extracurricular activities and fun over academics, I wasn't used to this level of rigor. Frustrated, I went to one of my professors and complained that Mom was acting like "Hitler." While the professor tried to maintain a straight face, I later realized how much her insistence helped me succeed. Her love might sometimes come across as strictness, but it's always rooted in what's best for us.

The bond between my parents and me is also reflected in how they've supported my dreams. I've always been a dreamer, and my parents have been my greatest allies in turning those dreams into reality. Their guidance and unwavering faith in me have been a source of strength, pushing me to aim higher and believe in myself.

—

Among the many cherished memories I hold, one that stands out the most is that as a small kid, my annual day dance performance to the song "Bhoomro" remains one of the proudest moments in my parents' lives. I had been chosen to perform the enchanting Kashmiri folk song. I vividly, remember the costume I wore, adorned with traditional embellishments that made me feel like a star. As, the music began, I stepped onto the stage, nervously at first, but soon, the rhythm took over, and I danced my little boy heart out.

They still talk about it with fondness to their friends, recalling how I cutely danced with unrestrained joy, completely oblivious to the spotlight but full of enthusiasm. They often say, "Kerfegar danced so cutely on that stage! It was like he was meant to perform." The laughter, the applause, and the beaming smile on my parents' faces as they watched me perform left an indelible mark on my heart. That performance, no matter how small or simple, meant the world to them, and it has since become a core memory that continues to bring us together during family conversations.

Similarly, in my boarding school, when I played a major role in the drama "The Trojan War: An Historical Comedy," my parents' pride was unmistakable. I remember them standing in the crowd as they watched me deliver my lines, and after the play, it wasn't just their smiles that told the story. It was the way other parents and teachers who came up to them, congratulating them on how well I had acted. People were impressed, not just by my performance, but by the confidence and poise I displayed. Their hearts swelled with pride, as they witnessed their little boy taking on the stage with such vigor.

For them, those moments were more than just performances; they were milestones in my journey, a reflection of the love and encouragement they had always given me.

Their marriage, their partnership, their way of supporting each other has been nothing short of inspirational. They have built a life centered around family, love, and values, and this has had a profound impact on Delara and me. Watching them over the years has taught us the essence of resilience, the importance of compromise, and the beauty of unconditional love.
Mom's helping nature and Dad's practicality are traits that complement each other beautifully. Whether it was sending food to someone in need or giving advice to friends and family members, their actions have always reflected their commitment to being good human beings. And then there's Dad, who has always been the silent rock in our lives. While Mom's actions often speak loudly, Dad's presence speaks volumes in quieter ways. He's the kind of person who believes in leading by example. Watching him work tirelessly for the family business and yet always making time for us has taught Delara and me what it means to be a provider, a protector, and a nurturer all at once.

I remember once asking Dad if he ever regretted giving up his career in interior design to return to Nashik and take over the family business. His answer has stayed with me: "No regrets, only love for my family." That one sentence encapsulates everything he stands for, a man who prioritizes his loved ones above all else, who finds joy in their happiness and fulfillment in their success. As Delara and I navigate our own paths in life, we carry with us the lessons our parents have taught us. Together, they've shown us what it means to build a life rooted in love, respect, and unwavering support.

———

And so, as I sit here reflecting on their journey, I feel
an overwhelming sense of gratitude. Gratitude for
their sacrifices, their teachings, and their love.
Gratitude for the countless ways they've enriched
our lives. But most of all, gratitude for the gift of
being their children. In them, we have seen the best
of what it means to be human, loving, selfless, and
kind. They are our heroes, our anchors, and our
greatest blessings.

Chapter 6: The Heirs of Heritage: A New Era of the Mistry's

It was a chilly evening in the dormitory of my boarding school, the kind of evening where the air felt heavier, and the silence seemed to stretch endlessly. I was sitting on my bunk bed, my legs curled up beneath me, clutching a letter from home. The envelope's familiar, neat handwriting immediately filled me with a sense of warmth and comfort, it was from my father. His script was always so deliberate, so steady, and I could almost hear his voice in every word he wrote. I tore open the envelope with excitement, eager for the updates that would bring a piece of home to the cold walls of the dormitory. But as I began to read, that familiar warmth quickly turned to a knot in my stomach.

The letter carried news that stopped me in my tracks. The last of my sisters, Sanaya, was moving out. She had been accepted to a prestigious university in the United States and would soon be flying across the ocean to begin her studies. My heart sank, and for a moment, the words blurred before me. As a sixth grader, the thought of Sanaya, the last of my sisters, leaving was overwhelming. Just a few short years ago, the house had been a lively whirlwind of noise, activity, and the comforting chaos of four sisters. But one by one, they were all leaving, and with each departure, I felt the house grow emptier and quieter.

Benaifer and Yasmin had already married, starting new chapters with their husbands, Yezdi and Mehernosh. Del-ara, who had always been my partner in mischief, was off to Pune for her studies, leaving me behind. And now, Sanaya, was about to step into a new world.

—

As a young boy, the thought of my sisters being taken away from me, scattered across different places, filled me with a profound sadness.
I couldn't fathom that I might never see them as often, that our bond might be stretched so thin. It felt like the family that had once been so tightly woven together was slowly unraveling. I was left behind, alone in a house that would soon be silent, with no one to fill the space but the memories.

Sitting there, with the letter still clutched in my hands, a wave of fear and loneliness washed over me. The house, once filled with laughter, shouting, and the simple, comforting presence of my sisters, would soon be a quieter place. It felt scary and unfamiliar. But as the reality sank in, I also realized just how deeply I loved them. My sisters weren't just siblings to me, they were my protectors, my friends, my confidants, and the very foundation of my world. I missed them already, even though they hadn't fully left yet. I missed Benaifer's careful attention to every detail, making sure I was ready for school. I missed Yasmin's quiet, unwavering strength that anchored me when things felt overwhelming. I missed Sanaya's vibrant energy that could light up a room, and Del-ara's unconditional love, always so freely given, no matter what.

That letter from my father marked the beginning of a new chapter not just for me, but for our entire family. Although we were now scattered across different cities and countries, I understood that the bond we shared, the love we had for one another, would never weaken. We were more than just siblings. We were a team, and no matter where life took us, that bond would remain unbroken. The house might have been growing quieter, but the love and support we had for each other would echo through the years, keeping us close even when we were far apart.

Growing up as the youngest in the Mistry family was nothing short of an adventure. We were five siblings: Benaifer, Yasmin, Sanaya, Del-ara, and me, Kerfegar. Each of us brought something unique to the family, and together we created a bond that was unbreakable. One of my fondest and earliest memories is of a blue or green scooter we had; a simple one you had to push with your legs to make it move. Being the "Kaccha Nimbu" of the family, my sisters always made it their mission to include me in their fun, even when I wasn't the most coordinated or quickest to catch on.

I remember one particular day, it might have been Yasmin's birthday or perhaps another sibling's celebration, when the house was filled with the buzz of family and friends. My sisters, in all their mischievous affection, decided the best way to entertain their little brother was to plop me onto the scooter. Taking turns, they'd either push me around or ride alongside me, their laughter echoing as we zipped through the hall. I can still feel the warm breeze on my face, hear their playful shrieks, and sense that indescribable feeling of being surrounded by their love.

They didn't care if I was the smallest or the slowest; to them, I was a part of every adventure. Those moments, small as they may seem, are etched in my heart as a reminder of how much my sisters cherished me, and how they made me feel like the most important "Kaccha Nimbu" in the world.

At the helm was Benaifer, the eldest and the wisest. She wasn't just our older sister; she was like a second mother to us. From the moment she was born, she became the darling of the family, the first grandchild after a long wait. Everyone doted on her, and she quickly became the center of attention.

—

My earliest memory of Benaifer was when she woke
me up for school one morning while Mom and Dad
were away. She helped me bathe, made me drink
my Bournvita, and sent me off to school like it was
the most natural thing in the world. She carried the
weight of being the eldest with grace, always looking
out for us. Even after she got married and moved to
Mumbai, she never stopped being our guide and
protector.

Then came Yasmin, the second eldest, who was the
calm strength of our family. She is said to be a
splitting image of our dear Silloo. While Benaifer led
with authority, Yasmin brought a sense of peace.
She had an unshakable patience and a way of
understanding everyone's emotions. Yasmin and
Benaifer shared a bond that was the envy of all of
us, it was always "Benu and Yasu," as if their names
were one. Yasmin was the one who would step in
quietly to help, always putting family first.

One of the happiest moments of my life was when
Yasmin and her husband Mehernosh gave us all our
little bundle of joy, Vaspar, making me an uncle for
the first time. Holding my little nephew in my arms, I
felt an overwhelming sense of joy and pride. Yasmin,
who had always been the quiet strength of our
family, had now brought a new life into the world,
and it was one of the most beautiful gifts she could
ever give this family. I also have a cherished
memory of her from when she was working in
Nashik. Back then, I wasn't allowed to have Kurkure
a newly launched snack or the Pepsi Ice Sticks that
all the kids loved. But Yasmin, being the doting sister
she was, would secretly bring them home from work
for me. I still remember the thrill of holding that cold
stick on a hot day, her mischievous smile as she
handed it to me, and the sense of pure joy it
brought. It's these little moments that show the
depth of her love and care for me.

—

Sanaya, the third sibling, is the vibrant one, full of energy and life. She is the bridge between the older and younger siblings, always finding a way to bring us together. Sanaya has a warmth about her that makes everyone feel special. Her enthusiasm is infectious, and she has a knack for making even the smallest moments memorable. One of the things I admire most about Sanaya is how well she knows me. She's the best gift giver in the family, always choosing the perfect thing that matches my tastes. It's as if she has an uncanny ability to read my mind, knowing exactly what I'd love.

What I cherish most, though, is the bond we share now. We both share a deep love for all things British, from planning elegant high teas at the Taj Mumbai to indulging in the most delicious Fortnum & Mason cookies and teas. Our taste in life is very much alike, we both appreciate the finer things in life, whether it's a perfectly brewed cup of Earl Grey or a beautifully set table for an afternoon tea.

Sanaya has a way of making every moment feel special, and some of my favorite memories with her are the times we spend together. Like the time she surprised me on my birthday by taking me out for Starbucks followed by a celebration and a long, leisurely drive afterward. It's not just about the coffee or the drive; it's about how she makes us all feel celebrated and loved. Sanaya's vibrant energy and her ability to connect on such a personal level make her so much more than a sibling, she's my confidant, my movie buddy, and someone who understands us all.

Then there is Del-ara, the one with an adventurous spirit and an energy that can light up the dullest room. She's the sporty one, the kind who'd dive headfirst into any game or challenge, while I am the classic nerd, content with a good book or scribbling away in my journal. Del-ara is the outgoing one, with a million friends who seem to adore her magnetic charm. In contrast, I am the quiet, introverted sibling, with a small but cherished circle of close friends.

Her zest for life is infectious, but oh, how she loves to trouble me! The most non-British thing about her, is her habit of shamelessly eating off my plate. Whether it's a piece of toast at breakfast or the last bite of dessert I've been saving, Del-ara swoops in with that mischievous grin, saying, "It tastes better from your plate!" Uff, that girl!

Beneath the pranks and antics, however, is someone deeply determined, a soul who knows exactly what she wants and won't rest until she achieves it. When Del-ara left for Pune for her studies, the house felt like it had lost its spark. The constant chatter, the physical fights we would have, the pulling of her long hair or the slapping games she would invent just to slap me and even the pranks, it all went silent. Without her around, things felt too quiet, almost as if the house had forgotten how to laugh. And yet, life without Del-ara's wild energy would be far too boring, and even though she eats off my plate, I wouldn't have her any other way.

And then there's me, the youngest of the Mistry siblings. Growing up with four older sisters meant that I was cared for, teased, and protected in equal measure. Each of them played a unique role in shaping me, and I am who I am today because of them.

—

Rakshabandhan has always held a special place in my heart, symbolizing the unspoken love and bond I share with my sisters. It's not just about the rituals or the gifts; it's about the deep connection that this festival represents. Every year, as my sisters tie a rakhi around my wrist, I feel a sense of protection and warmth that words can't describe. Since 5th grade, I've kept every rakhi given to me by my sisters. These simple threads, tied with love, carry memories of our shared moments and the promises we've made to each other.

Though life has taken us in different directions, the rakhi's remain a tangible reminder of our unbreakable bond. They hold more meaning than just tradition; they represent the laughter, the love, and the comfort I've always found in my family. I've kept them all, carefully stored away. Whenever I feel distant or down, I open that box, and the rakhi's remind me of the deep connection we share. Even if I don't say it often, these rakhi's mean the world to me.

Even now, as adults with our own families and responsibilities, the love we have for each other is unshakable. We are the heirs of a rich legacy, carrying forward the traditions and values of the Mistry's while creating a new era of our own. And no matter where life takes us, I know that the connection we share will always bring us back to each other. These are the Mistry siblings, Benaifer, Yasmin, Sanaya, Del-ara, and me, we are a story of love, laughter, and the legacy we carry forward together. We are the heirs of heritage, and this is our new era.

Chapter 7: My Brother-in-Laws, Yezdi and Mehernosh

Yezdi and Mehernosh are not just my brother-in-laws; they are two individuals who, in their own unique ways, left a lasting impression on me from the moment they entered my life. Both came into our family during an important time in my childhood, and the way they each introduced themselves remains etched in my memory.

I was in fourth grade when both Yezdi and Mehernosh became a part of our family. Yezdi, the elder of the two, married my oldest sister, Benaifer. It was a momentous occasion. Benaifer was the first daughter in our family to get married in a long, long time, and it felt like we were handing over a precious gem to another family. This wasn't just a wedding; it was a transition, a symbol of change. The family had a sense of pride and bittersweet sadness as we gave a send-off to Benaifer. The wedding itself was a grand affair, filled with music, laughter, and the usual wedding chaos. I remember how Yezdi looked that day, dressed in a sharp white dugli, with a warm smile that made everyone around him feel at ease. Despite the formalities, he had a way of making the entire atmosphere lighter, almost as if he was a part of the family for much longer than he actually was. I distinctly recall my first impression of him. He was kind, approachable, and carried himself with a quiet confidence. What stood out the most, however, was his generosity.

On that first day we met, Yezdi gifted me a small set of stationery, a notepad and a pen along with a train set. I was young, and at the time, I thought of it as just another gift. But as I grew older, I realized how thoughtful that gift was.

It wasn't just something bought from a store; it was something he picked out with care, knowing that I was a kid who loved to colour and I had just started to develop a keen interest in trains. His attention to detail, to me as an individual, was something I would come to appreciate even more as I got older.

A year later came Yasmin's wedding to Mehernosh. This was another significant event in our family. Yasmin, my second sister, was a bright and loving spirit, and it was no surprise that she was also given away to another family with as much love as Benaifer. The wedding was yet another celebration of love, but it also marked the beginning of a new chapter for me, as it was the second wedding of a sister in such a short span of time. The house that once hosted these girls now felt empty without them.

Now, it might sound a bit confusing, but there are two Mehernosh's in our family. This Mehernosh was the one who married Yasmin, he was a bit quieter and more reserved at first. He had a different presence, one that didn't demand attention but earned it gradually with his actions. I remember being slightly nervous the first time I met him, but just like Yezdi, he quickly made me feel comfortable. He wasn't just another family member; he was someone who genuinely cared for us.

I was once playing in the passage of our house when Mehernosh saw me struggling to fix a yellow skateboard that had a loose piece. Without any hesitation, he knelt down beside me and, in his calm manner, helped me put it back together. It wasn't just about fixing the toy; it was about his willingness to engage, to be a part of my world for that brief moment. His calm demeanor and gentle nature were comforting, and even as a child, I could sense that he genuinely cared.

—

In the years that followed, I witnessed the way both of them supported my sisters through thick and thin. Yezdi, with his infectious energy, was always ready with a joke or a lighthearted comment, making even the toughest of situations seem bearable. He had a way of balancing the serious with the playful, never allowing the weight of life's challenges to overshadow the lighter moments. He would often tell stories of his childhood, many of them humorous and heartwarming, which kept our spirits high even during family gatherings.

Mehernosh, on the other hand, was a man of few words but immense depth. He didn't need to speak much, his actions spoke louder than anything he could say. Whether it was making sure everyone was well-fed at family dinners or offering a quiet word of encouragement when someone was struggling, he was the steady presence in the room. I admired his ability to listen without judgment and to offer advice that was both practical and compassionate.

There are moments in life that stay with you forever, moments filled with laughter, excitement, and a sense of freedom. One of those unforgettable times was when I went to Bordi with Yasmin and Mehernosh as a 11-year-old kid. It was a trip that, even years later, I think back on with so much joy and fondness. Bordi, with its tranquil beaches and peaceful atmosphere, felt like the perfect getaway. Yasmin and Mehernosh, as usual, made sure I had the time of my life. Yasmin, ever the fun-loving sister, was more than happy to let me run around the homestay and explore the beach. I remember running freely along the shoreline, the sand between my toes and the cool sea breeze against my face. It felt like the world had slowed down, and for those few hours, I could just be a kid, without a care in the world.

—

Meanwhile, Mehernosh, ever calm and collected, sat on the porch, playing on my PSP (PlayStation Portable). I had brought it along with me, and Mehernosh seemed genuinely interested in trying it out. He had always been quiet and reserved, but when he picked up the PSP and started playing, I saw a different side of him. He wasn't just a quiet observer; he was someone who could get fully immersed in something. It was a simple but meaningful moment that made me realize how much I valued the small things we did together.

Later that day, Yasmin and I sat down to have a little fun of our own. I had been playing on the PSP for a while, and Yasmin, curious as ever, wanted to learn how to play. At first, she fumbled with the controls, her thumbs unsure of where to go. But with some patience, I managed to teach her the basics. It was a funny sight, Yasmin trying to figure out the game, her playful comments making the whole experience even more enjoyable. Eventually, she got the hang of it, and we spent hours playing together, laughing over small victories and learning how to strategize.

But, as with any trip, there were also moments of challenge. During dinner, Yasmin insisted that I eat a vegetable, something I was notoriously picky about. She had this look of determination in her eyes, as if she were on a mission to make me eat it, and her teasing was relentless. "You'll like it, just try it!" she said, pushing the plate toward me. I knew I couldn't get away with refusing, so I forced myself to take a bite. It was one of those moments where I had to swallow my pride (and the vegetable) to avoid hearing her endless banter. And to my surprise, it wasn't as bad as I had imagined. Yasmin, of course, had a victory look on her face, which I grudgingly acknowledged.

Another unforgettable experience was when Benaifer and Yezdi took me out to TGI Friday's. I think I must have been around 14 or 15 at the time, and it felt like the most exciting outing. We sat down in the cozy booth, the air buzzing with the sounds of laughter and clinking glasses. The food, as always, was delicious, but the highlight of the meal was the competition that unfolded between Benaifer and me. We had ordered iced tea, and as always, I was trying to finish my glass as quickly as possible. Benaifer, always up for a challenge, decided to compete with me. We sipped our iced teas as fast as we could, laughing as we raced to the finish line. Of course, being the older sister, Benaifer was the first to finish, but I didn't mind. The real fun was in the rivalry and the laughter that followed.

That trip to TGI Friday's was just another example of how my time with Yezdi and Benaifer was filled with lighthearted moments. Yezdi, sitting there with a content smile, was as supportive as ever, enjoying the banter between Benaifer and me. He wasn't just the husband of my sister; he was my brother, my friend, and someone who made family moments so much more enjoyable. His calm presence balanced out Benaifer's playful energy, creating a perfect mix of fun and relaxation.

Speaking of family moments, there was the time when Benaifer and Yezdi took me shopping for my birthday clothes. My mother had asked them to help me pick something out, and, as usual, I was being incredibly fussy. I had a vision in my head of what I wanted but couldn't quite find it. I remember feeling frustrated, unable to decide what would be perfect. Benaifer, ever patient, would offer suggestions, while Yezdi, not one to rush, would calmly suggest, "Maybe we can try another store."

—

They didn't rush me, which I appreciated. After what felt like hours, I finally settled on a shirt, but not before I had driven them both nearly crazy with indecision.

Looking back, these moments, whether running on the beach with Yasmin, playing on the PSP with Mehernosh, racing Benaifer to finish iced tea, or shopping for clothes with Yezdi, are among the most cherished memories of my childhood. It was during these times that I realized how lucky I was to have such wonderful people in my life. Yezdi and Mehernosh, each in their own way, helped shape my understanding of what it means to be part of a family. They were more than just my brother-in-laws, they were companions, mentors, and, above all, friends.

Both Yezdi and Mehernosh played crucial roles in shaping the person I am today. They taught me the value of generosity, the importance of action over words, and the quiet strength of being there for those you love. They weren't just my brother-in-law's, they were role models, mentors, and above all, family. Their stories, their kindness, and their steady presence in our lives are something I will always treasure. They entered my life as my sisters' husbands, but over the years, they became something much more, guiding figures in my journey of growing up. They taught me that family is not just about blood relations; it's about the connections we form, the love we share, and the support we offer one another.

Chapter 8: The Unexpected Guests: Thieves, Robbers, Gunmen, and Hypnosis

Our family home has always been a magnet for stories, some heartwarming, others downright terrifying. Over the years, it has welcomed family, friends, celebrities, and even thieves, robbers, and conmen. These unexpected guests have left behind tales that, while unsettling at the time, have become a testament to the resilience, quick thinking, and courage of our family.

One of the most vivid stories from our home began with an unsettling mystery. For several days, small amounts of cash, Rs. 50 here, Rs. 100 there, would go missing from the counter of our shop. Dad initially thought it was a mistake or oversight by the staff, but when the pattern continued, he and Mom decided to investigate. Night after night, they stayed awake, glued to the CCTV footage, determined to catch the culprit.

Then, late one night, Mom noticed something shocking on the live feed. Around 3 a.m., a man was sneaking into the shop through a small opening in the cashier's counter. She immediately shouted for Dad, and the two of them sprang into action. They woke up Rati Kaki and Polly Kaka and armed with a hockey stick and a walking stick, they blocked the thief's escape route and called the police. As the police arrived and entered the shop, they were met with an eerie sight, no thief in sight. After a frantic search, Dad discovered a hole in the wooden wall connecting the shop to our home. Fear gripped everyone as they realized the thief had made his way into the house, where Delara, and I were fast asleep.

—

Mom, Dad, and the police rushed into the house, searching every corner for the intruder. When they reached my room, they woke me with panicked cries of "Kerfegar, wake up! There's a thief in the house!" Groggy and confused, I stumbled into the hall, only to find a dozen police officers searching every nook and cranny of our home. Finally, the thief was found hiding behind gunny bags in the passageway. He was apprehended, but the memory of that night remains etched in all our minds, a chaotic mix of fear and relief.

The stories don't end there. Long before my time, during my grandfather Jamshed's era, the family was thrust into an unforgettable and terrifying ordeal. It was a quiet, eerie night, midnight to be exact. The full moon hung low in the sky, casting an almost ghostly glow over the estate. The trees outside swayed gently in the cool night breeze, their shadows stretching long across the ground. Everyone in the house was deep in sleep, unaware of the danger approaching. It was in the stillness of this peaceful night that Bawa first heard the knock at the door, a sound that would change everything.

With careful steps, Jamshed approached the door, which had a small panel for speaking to visitors. Through this modest opening, two men dressed as policemen spoke in calm, authoritative tones. They claimed to have crucial information about a robbery targeting the house, and their uniformed presence seemed convincing. Though the night air was heavy with the kind of silence that makes every sound seem amplified, Jamshed, ever the cautious man, kept his wits about him. He engaged with them, speaking through the small panel door, trying to gather more details, sensing there was something off in their demeanor.

—

Without warning, one of the men suddenly threw a white powder through the window, hoping to incapacitate Bawa and carry out their plan. Their goal was clear, they intended to enter under the false pretense of authority, catching the family off guard. But my grandfather was sharp and vigilant. As the powder filled the air, Jamshed's instincts took over. He immediately raised the alarm, shouting loudly for his wife, brother, and sister to wake up. The men, realizing their plan had failed, fled quickly into the night, their footsteps lost in the darkness. Though the family was shaken, they were unharmed, and the harrowing event served as a powerful reminder that, in the dead of night, under the cover of shadows, appearances can be deceiving, and trusting one's instincts is crucial for survival.

Years later, our fearless Mahrukh Kaki and Mehernosh Kaka would find themselves facing the most terrifying danger our family has ever encountered. It was just an ordinary night, or so they thought. After closing the doors of Mistry Liquor Mart for the day, they set out to drive home with the day's cash securely in hand. The streets were quiet, the air cool, and the rhythmic hum of the car engine was the only sound. However, as they drove through the familiar roads toward their home, they began to notice something unsettling, a group of young men on bikes, their presence growing more noticeable as they seemed to follow the car at a steady pace. At first, Kaki and Kaka thought little of it, dismissing it as mere coincidence. But the eerie sense of being watched gradually turned into something far more sinister. As they approached their neighborhood, the bikers closed in, and before they knew it, the car was surrounded. Panic surged through them as the men began to block their path, and the once quiet evening transformed into a nightmare.

—

One of the bikers pulled out a gun, pointing it directly at them with a cold, menacing stare. "Hand over the cash, or we'll shoot!" he yelled, his voice dripping with threat. In an instant, the car door was yanked open, and the assailants demanded the bag of money. Kaki, however, was not one to be intimidated. True to her fiery spirit and unyielding courage, she refused to let go of the bag, even with the gun aimed at her. Her defiance caught the attackers off guard, momentarily stalling them. But that hesitation didn't last long. Without warning, one of the robbers fired a shot into the ground, the deafening sound of it breaking the tense silence and sending a clear message.

Realizing the gravity of the situation, Kaki, though shaken, knew she had no choice. Reluctantly, she handed over the cash, understanding that her own safety was paramount. The robbers, now satisfied with their haul, fled into the night, leaving behind a shaken but unharmed Kaka and Kaki. As soon as the danger passed, the couple immediately called the police, and a citywide manhunt for the culprits began. Days later, the criminals were apprehended, and the ordeal came to a close.

Kaki's bravery in the face of such a threat became the stuff of family legend, a tale that has been passed down through the generations. Her courage, resilience, and unwavering spirit in those critical moments would forever be remembered as an inspiring testament to the strength and bravery that runs through our bloodline.

But perhaps the most devastating incident occurred when I was in college. One evening, two men were smoking a joint outside our shop when a heated argument escalated into violence. One of the men stabbed the other with a knife, leaving him seriously injured.

The victim was rushed to the hospital, but a misunderstanding ensued when the injured man's family assumed the altercation had taken place inside our shop and blamed us for not intervening. Fueled by rage, around 12 men stormed into our shop late that night, seeking revenge. Their fury was unleashed as they looted the shop, breaking counters and glass, smashing bottles, and ransacking the cash register. Employees were caught off guard; some panicked and hid behind boxes, while others ran for their lives. A few managed to climb onto the roof, shouting for help.

Our home, with its unique architectural design, had an opening in the center that connected indirectly to the shop. This allowed us to guide the employees into the house for safety, shielding them from further harm. Meanwhile, the attackers continued their rampage, inflicting damage not just on the shop but also on the staff who couldn't escape. Eventually, the men fled, leaving behind a trail of destruction. The police were called, and an investigation began. Although the culprits were apprehended, only about 40% of the stolen money was ever recovered. The incident shook our family to its core, a stark reminder of the vulnerability of both our home and our livelihood.

The most unique and baffling story, however, involved hypnosis, a phenomenon none of us had ever encountered before. When Dad first took over running the shop, he was supported by Mom, Fuiji, and Minoo Kaka. At the time, there was a severe shortage of coins, so we relied on a man who regularly delivered bags of coins to the shop.

The arrangement seemed simple enough: the man would bring coins, which were counted, and he was paid in cash.

However, Fuiji began noticing discrepancies, insisting that the number of coins seemed fewer than what we were paying for. Dad initially dismissed her concerns, thinking it was a counting error due to her age. But she kept on insisting that something seemed to be going wrong somewhere.

But something about the man's behavior caught Dad's attention. He always insisted that my mom, who wore spectacles, not count the coins. Instead, he preferred Dad or one of the shop boys to do it. Curious, Dad decided to investigate further. What he discovered was shocking: the man was hypnotizing them.

Using a technique known as "nazarbandi" in Hindi, he manipulated their perception, making them believe there were 150 coins in the bag when, in reality, there were only 100. My mom's spectacles, it turned out, made her immune to hypnosis, which is why the man avoided her counting. Realizing the scam, the family reported the man to the police. They learned this was part of a larger operation targeting shopkeepers in the city. While the incident was unsettling, it taught the family the importance of vigilance and trusting one another's instincts.

Each of these incidents, though frightening, has become part of our family's shared narrative. From the thief in the shop to the conmen at the door, Kaki's brave encounter with armed robbers, the violent misunderstanding, and the hypnosis scam, these stories remind us of the strength, unity, and love that define us. Our home is more than just a building; it is a silent witness to the trials and triumphs of our family, a place where courage and resilience thrive, even in the most unexpected moments.

—

Through all these moments of turmoil and uncertainty, our home has stood as more than just a shelter, it has been the heartbeat of our family, a place that absorbs every joy, fear, triumph, and sorrow. Its walls have heard the laughter of children, the whispers of hope, and the cries of despair, and they carry the echoes of lives lived with courage and conviction.

Each story, no matter how harrowing, became a thread in the tapestry of our shared existence, binding us closer together. As we sat around the dinner table recounting these events, there was an unspoken bond that strengthened with every tale, a bond forged in the fires of experience and tempered with love and understanding.

Chapter 9: A Tale of Two Dogs – Jenny and Max

Dogs have a way of becoming more than just animals, they weave themselves into the lives and hearts of the people around them. In our family, Jenny, the gentle matriarch of my childhood, and Max, the wild, hyperactive protector of our present, have shaped so many memories. While my relationship with them has always been complicated by my fear of dogs, their bond with my sister Delara has been nothing short of extraordinary.

Jenny was the epitome of calm. She was an old, dignified lady who carried herself with grace. Her soft eyes seemed to understand everything, and her gentle nature endeared her to everyone in the family. To me, Jenny was the perfect dog, respectful of boundaries and quiet in her affection. She would spend her days lounging in the sun, occasionally lifting her head to acknowledge someone passing by. At night, she would curl up in a corner, her presence as comforting as a warm blanket.

Everyone loved Jenny. Even I, with my irrational fear of dogs, found her soothing. She never barked unnecessarily or startled anyone with sudden movements. If she noticed my fear, she never acted on it. Instead, she seemed to keep her distance out of respect, as if to say, "I'm here if you need me, but I won't bother you." For Delara, though, Jenny was more than just a dog, she was her first real companion. When Jenny passed away, it felt like we'd lost a family member. For Delara, it was a particularly hard loss. Jenny had been her confidant and friend, and her absence was deeply felt.

I thought that was the end of our family's relationship with dogs. But Delara's love for them couldn't be contained for long. Soon, Max entered our lives, and everything changed.

Max is as different from Jenny as night is from day. A dog with boundless energy, he is a hyperactive whirlwind of barking, leaping, and running. He seems to have no concept of personal space, and his enthusiasm for life is both infectious and terrifying, at least to me. Max greets every visitor with a booming bark and a wagging tail that could knock over a small child. He's Delara's dog through and through, and their bond is one of unbridled energy and mutual understanding.

If Jenny was a soothing presence, Max is a chaotic force of nature. His barking echoes through the house at the slightest hint of activity outside, a passing car, a bird on the wall, or even a rustling leaf. Delara, of course, loves this about him. She calls him "my crazy boy" and spends hours playing fetch with him, teaching him commands, and laughing at his antics. Watching them together is like watching two best friends who are perfectly in sync with each other's madness.

Max is not just hyperactive, though, he's also a bit of a biter. He loves to bite anything and everything in sight, making him a constant challenge to handle. His biting and constant barking, sometimes for hours on end, are part of the whirlwind that is his personality. Because of Max's uncontrollable nature, I've had to use a different entry and exit to the house than the rest of the family. I'm always on high alert because Max will lunge at anything that moves.

I've even gotten a bit mischievous with him, sometimes, from my room, I'll randomly bark or make cat noises just to upset him, watching him go into a frenzy. I know, I know, I'm a bit naughty too. But it's all in good fun.

There was also this one time when I was playing loud music in my room, and Max, of all things, sat outside on the veranda, listening to the music as if it were his personal concert. It was strange, yet kind of funny.

But it's not all chaos with Max. I also wanted to see his loyalty towards me. One day, when no one else was home, I decided to test him. I thought, "What would Max do if an intruder were to break in?" So, I started shouting, "Help! Help! Help!" from inside the house, hoping to see if he would come running to my aid. But instead of charging to my rescue, all Max did was turn around, give me a stern look as if to say, "Stop it, you annoying kid," and then went back to his usual antics. I guess I misjudged the situation, Max had no time for my dramatics.

For me, however, Max is a constant challenge. His energy and unpredictability make me uneasy, and his booming bark can send me scrambling for cover. He seems to sense my fear but is far too excitable to adjust his behavior. Instead, he often barrels toward me, only to be called back by Delara's stern voice. "Kerfegar, he just wants to play!" she says, laughing, but my heart races every time.

Despite my fear, I can't deny that Max has a good heart. There are moments when his wildness subsides, and I see the loyal, loving companion Delara adores. Like the time he stood guard by the gate all night when he sensed something unusual outside, or when he lay quietly by Delara's side after a particularly hard day. His loyalty is unwavering, and his bond with Delara is a reminder of how dogs, no matter their personality, can bring immense joy and comfort to those who love them.

Jenny and Max are two sides of the same coin, one calm and serene, the other wild and exuberant. While Jenny taught us the beauty of quiet companionship, Max has shown us the power of unrestrained energy and love. For Delara, they have been best friends and kindred spirits. For me, they've been lessons in patience, understanding, and the surprising ways dogs can touch our lives, even when we're scared of them. Through them, I've come to realize that dogs, whether calm like Jenny or wild like Max, bring something invaluable to a family, a sense of connection, love, and shared memories that last a lifetime.

Chapter 10: Tulsi Bai the Heart of our Home

Every family has its unsung hero, the one whose presence is so deeply woven into the fabric of daily life that it becomes impossible to imagine the home without them. For the Mistry family, that hero was Tulsi Bai. She wasn't related to us by blood, but she was family in every sense of the word. Her story, humble and remarkable, begins when she was just a small girl cutting wood near our home, unaware of the destiny that awaited her. It was my great-grandmother, Shirinibai, who first spotted her. The young girl, frail yet spirited, was hard at work, cutting trees with an intensity that belied her age. Seeing her plight and sensing something special about her, Shirinibai took her in, not just as a house help but as someone who would soon become an indispensable part of the household. And so, Tulsi Bai began her journey with the Mistry family.

Over the years, she grew with us, in many ways shaping the rhythm of our home. She wasn't just a cook or a cleaner; she was a keeper of secrets, a bearer of traditions, and a silent witness to the joys and sorrows that unfolded under our roof. She had a way of understanding people like no one else. Whether it was my father's preference for vegetarian food, my uncle's sweet tooth, or my grandmother Silloo's penchant for perfectly brewed tea, Tulsi Bai knew it all. She had a remarkable memory, too. She never needed reminders about anyone's dietary restrictions or allergies. If someone in the family couldn't eat nuts or didn't like a certain vegetable, she'd remember it for years without anyone ever needing to repeat it. It wasn't just her job; it was her way of caring.

But it wasn't always smooth sailing. Tulsi Bai had a fiery side, and this often led to playful spats with my grandmother, Silloo.

———

Their arguments were legendary, often resembling the kind of bickering you'd see between sisters. They would stop talking to each other for days, stubbornly ignoring each other's presence, much to the amusement of everyone else in the family.
Yet, even in their silence, there was a deep bond. Eventually, one of them would give in, and things would return to normal, their affection for each other stronger than ever.

One of the most touching stories I've heard about Tulsi Bai is from my own Navjot ceremony. For those unfamiliar, a Navjot is a sacred initiation ceremony in Zoroastrian tradition, marking the beginning of one's spiritual journey. It's a momentous occasion for any family, and mine was no different. Amidst all the preparations and excitement, Tulsi Bai made a special request to my parents. "Buy me a nice saree," she said, "so I can wear it on Kerfegar's Navjot." My parents, recognizing the depth of her love for the family, and agreed without hesitation. They didn't just buy her a saree; they told her to choose the most beautiful and expensive one she wanted. For someone like Tulsi Bai, who had lived a life of simplicity, this gesture meant the world. She picked a saree that was radiant, rich in color, and perfect for the occasion. On the day of my Navjot, she wore it with unmatched pride, moving around the house with a sense of joy and accomplishment that was palpable to everyone.

Years later, when Tulsi Bai passed away, her daughter shared something that brought tears to our eyes. She told us that her mother had cherished that saree so deeply that she chose to wear it on her final journey. She was adorned in it when she was placed on the funeral pyre, a testament to how much that gesture from my parents had meant to her.

———

That saree wasn't just a piece of clothing; it was a symbol of her place in our family and the love and respect we had for her.

Even after her passing, her connection to our family continued. Tulsi Bai's daughter and granddaughters carried forward her legacy, working for us with the same dedication and care that defined her. Their presence reminded us of the strength and love that had been a hallmark of her life, ensuring that her spirit remained alive in our home.

Tulsi Bai's passing left a void that could never be filled. She was the last of a generation that truly understood the nuances of our home. She had seen my uncles and father grow into young men, watched as my cousins and I transformed from mischievous children to young adults, and witnessed the evolution of the Mistry family over decades.

There's a certain magic to the way she cared for everyone. She was more than a house help; she was a caretaker of hearts. She celebrated our milestones, mourned our losses, and remained a constant in a world that was always changing. Even when she disagreed with someone or had one of her rare outbursts, her loyalty to the family never wavered. In many ways, she was a bridge between the past and the present. She carried stories of a time when life was simpler, when my great-grandmother Shirinibai was the matriarch, and the house was bustling with activity. She would tell us tales of those days, her eyes lighting up as she recounted memories of festivals, family gatherings, and everyday moments that had become cherished history.

For me, Tulsi Bai represents something invaluable, the kind of unconditional love and devotion that is increasingly rare in today's world. She didn't have to care about our likes and dislikes or go out of her way to make sure we were happy. But she did, because that's who she was. As I look back on her life and the impact she had on our family, I realize that there truly was, and never will be, anyone like her. She was one of a kind, a woman of incredible strength, compassion, and loyalty. Her legacy lives on in the stories we tell, the traditions we uphold, and the values she exemplified every single day.

The Mistry home may have changed over the years, but the spirit of people like Tulsi Bai remains embedded in its walls, in its memories, and in the hearts of those who were fortunate enough to know her.

Chapter 11: A Sister's Goodbye: Love Wrapped in Sorrow

THIS CHAPTER IS A GOODBYE LETTER FROM ME TO MY DEAR SISTER BENAIFER WHO IS CURRENTLY IN PALLIATIVE CARE DUE TO CANCER.

My Dearest Benaifer,

It feels almost impossible to put into words what I'm feeling right now, knowing how close we are to saying goodbye. The thought of a life without you feels unbearable, and yet, here I am, trying to write this letter, something I never thought I'd have to do.

When I think of you, my heart fills with warmth and gratitude for all the memories we've created together. Your last visit to Nashik will forever remain one of my most cherished moments. Sitting together, laughing, and relishing the hot sabudana vadas you love so much, the comforting dhai chawal Mahrukh Kaki made, and the khan ni rotli that reminded us of our good old days, it all felt so perfect. I remember the joy on your face when we drove out with Sanaya to Trimbak, taking in the fresh air and serene views, or the day we spent exploring Ama Trails and that nice cup of coffee we had. Those small outings meant the world to me because I got to see you smile, even when you were fighting through so much pain.

The house feels so quiet now, Benu. It's as if it knows that soon, you'll no longer be with us. We all feel this heaviness, this ache that refuses to leave. But what keeps us going is the incredible strength and love you've shown us throughout your life. You've been the anchor holding this family together, the one who always made sure everyone was cared for and loved.

Benu, you weren't just a sister to me, you were a warrior, a Sherni. Do you remember when I first called you that? It was during one of your toughest days in this battle against cancer.
You were to have your first chemotherapy session, and we video called you saying everything will be okay but instead of letting the pain break you, you smiled, stood tall, and said, "yes, I know."
It was in that moment I realized that your spirit was unshakable. You refused to let this illness define you, standing firm like a lioness protecting her pride, ready to face any storm.

You didn't just fight this battle; you taught all of us what resilience truly looks like. Even when the pain was unbearable, you carried yourself with dignity, never once letting us see the depth of your suffering. You shielded us, Benu, like a true Sherni. Your roars weren't loud; they were silent and steady, reminding us to never give up, to face every challenge with courage, and to find strength even in the darkest times.

Even on days when the world felt heavy, your smile could light up the room. That's the kind of lioness you were, brave, fearless, and full of love. You fought not just for yourself but for all of us, making sure we knew that no matter what, you were there, leading the way, showing us how to be strong.

I will carry your lessons with me forever. Every time life throws me a challenge, I'll think of you, my fierce, loving Sherni. I'll think of how you never backed down, how you faced everything with grace and determination. You've set an example for all of us, Benu, one that I'll strive to live up to for the rest of my life. It hurts, Benu. It really does. I know it's not your fault, but I can't help feeling this deep sense of loss. You have always been the sweetheart of this family.

And it's not just me who feels this way. Polly Kaka and Rati Kaki have been so brave, but I can see the sorrow in their eyes. Their eldest child, their beloved Benu, is slipping away, and it's breaking them piece by piece.

I want to tell you how proud I am of Yezdi. He too has been a pillar of strength, standing by you through every challenge, ensuring that you were comfortable and loved every single day. He has shown me what it truly means to be a devoted husband. I could not have asked for a better brother-in-law. Knowing that you've had him by your side gives me a small sense of peace in this heartbreaking time.

Benu, I think about Yasmin too. How lost she will feel without you. It was always "Benu and Yasu," the inseparable sisters. Ever since we were children, the two of you were like two sides of the same coin, always together, always in sync. The bond you shared was something truly special. You were not just her older sister; you were her confidante, her best friend, her second mother.
Now, it will just be Yasu, carrying the weight of your absence. I can already see how much she's struggling with the thought of losing you. She keeps trying to be strong for the rest of us, but I know she's breaking inside. That bond, that sisterhood, feels incomplete without you, and I don't know how any of us will ever fill the void you're leaving behind. I know Yasmin will try her best to honor your memory, to be the sister you always believed she could be, but it won't be the same without her Benu by her side.

Benu, you have the most wonderful parents, sisters, and husband who have stood by you through it all. And me, your little brother, who loves you more than words can ever express.

The thought of not being able to hear your voice, to see your smile, to share those little moments with you, it's devastating. But even in this pain, I am comforted by the knowledge that you will finally be at peace, free from the suffering you've endured so bravely.

I know you'll be in good hands up there, with Fuiji, Minoo Kaka, and the rest of our family who have been waiting to embrace you again. And most of all, I know Silloo and Jamshed will be overjoyed to reunite with their first granddaughter. You will finally get to meet your mother-in-law and father-in-law and be safe, loved, and surrounded by family, just as you have always been here with us.

I'll miss you, Benu, more than I can ever say. Thank you for being the incredible sister, guide, and friend that you've been to me. Thank you for all the love, laughter, and memories you've given us. You will always be in my heart, in every corner of this house, in every story we share about you.

Goodbye, my darling Sherni. I love you more than words can describe.

Forever your little brother,

Kerfegar

(Benaifer passed away on the 21st of December 2024, surrounded by her husband, parents, and sister.)

Chapter 12: The Story of Benaifer

Benaifer was the first sibling, born in 1977. The first child of Polly Kaka and Rati Kaki, the first grandchild of Silloo and Jamshed, and the first little cutie pie of the Mistry family. After years, she was the first baby born into our family and, naturally, the center of attention. I imagine her arrival brought so much joy that the house must have felt like a festival, laughter, light, and a constant stream of visitors. She wasn't just the darling of the Mistry family; she was adored by everyone. A young, dashing baby girl, already charming the world with her presence.

My earliest memory of her isn't grand or dramatic. It was a quiet, beautiful morning when Mom and Dad were out, and I had to go to school. It was Benaifer who woke me up, her soft voice gently pulling me out of my sleep. I must have been such a groggy little thing, stumbling about, but she managed it all. She bathed me, combed my unruly hair, and made me drink Bournvita while Minoo Kaka looked on, probably amused at the whole scene. Then she sent me off to school, just like any older sister would. Even at that young age, she had a maturity about her, a sense of responsibility that came naturally. Looking back now, I see how lucky I was to have her.

As the youngest rascal of the lot, I would often barge into Kaki's room while Benu and Yasmin studied for their exams. She'd be completely immersed in her books when I'd walk in, innocent and wide-eyed, and ask her to play with me. It must have been so frustrating for her and Yasu. Their younger brother interrupting them when they were trying to focus. And yet, sometimes, both would give in, closing their books just to keep me happy. I think, even then, they understood that this small boy just wanted to be around his sisters.

When she got married to Yezdi, I didn't quite
understand what was happening. The house was
buzzing with excitement, filled with guests and
relatives, and I turned to Delara, to ask why there
were so many people. Delara, being Delara, couldn't
resist pulling a prank on me.

 "They're here to kidnap her," she said with a
straight face. "Yezdi is marrying her and kidnapping
her to Mumbai." For two months, two whole months
I believed that Yezdi had kidnapped my sister. My
little mind couldn't process why someone would
kidnap her and I remember feeling so upset until
Mom finally sat me down and explained what
marriage was. Thanks, Delara, for scarring me!

Some memories stick with you, no matter how small
they seem. I remember visiting Benaifer at her in-
laws' house not long after she got married. A group
of us kids were playing, and we started jumping on
the bed in her room. We were having the time of our
lives until, crack! , the bed broke right under us. I
froze, absolutely terrified. I was sure that my
parents would find out and I'd get scolded for life.
But Benaifer swooped in, like she always did. She
looked at me and smiled. "Don't worry," she said,
"it's okay. Anyway, the bed was too small for us."
That was Benaifer, calm, reassuring, and always on
my side. She saved me that day, as she did so many
other times.

Years later, when I was living in Mumbai, I went
through a tough time. I stayed as a paying guest,
and the landlady was no less than a nightmare. She
fed me food that was seven or eight days old, turned
off the fan at night in the sweltering Mumbai heat,
and even switched off the lights when I was
studying.

I remember feeling completely helpless, miserable, and alone. One day, I couldn't take it anymore and went to Benaifer's house in tears. I sat there, crying and venting about everything I'd been going through. She sat with me, listening to every word I said, every detail of my struggle. She let me get it all out. And when I was done, she smiled that mischievous smile of hers and said, "Do you want me to go to her house and fix the lady who's bothering my little brother?"

That's what she did, she took away the heaviness in my heart with her humor, her love, and her unshakable support. She couldn't stand to see me suffer. She would send Yezdi out to bring me little treats, like vada pav, pav bhaji or invite me over for tea, just to cheer me up. Those small gestures meant the world to me. It wasn't about the food; it was about knowing that someone cared.

Eventually, I moved out of that dreadful place into a private apartment, but the story didn't end there. You see, Benaifer held a quiet grudge against that landlady. Even years later, whenever she saw her in the colony, she would ignore her completely, turning her face away as though she didn't exist. I'd laugh and tell her to let it go, but she never did. "No one troubles my little brother and gets away with it," she would say. That was my sister, fiercely protective, even in the smallest of things.

Living in Mumbai also brought some beautiful days spent with her and Yezdi. There was this famous thali place in town that we loved. It became our little tradition, the three of us sitting down for a hearty meal and then going for long walks in the charming old streets nearby.

There are so many memories like these, small, beautiful moments that remind me of the bond we shared. She worried about me, cared for me, and always, always had my back. Even when life took us in different directions, her love never wavered.

She had a way of making everything feel okay. Whether it was saving me from scoldings, listening to my problems, or simply teasing me to make me laugh, she knew exactly what to do. Her love was constant, something I could always rely on, no matter how old I got or how far I went. And it wasn't just me. She was the glue that held us all together, her parents, her siblings, and later, her own family with Yezdi. She poured so much love into every role she played. A daughter, sister, wife, and friend. And in every one of those roles, she gave all of herself, never holding back.

Even when her health began to falter, she carried herself with grace, courage, and an unyielding spirit. Her battle with cancer was nothing short of inspiring. She faced it with strength and dignity, fighting every step of the way. Even in the toughest moments, she managed to find light and humor, reassuring us that she was okay. She was determined not to let her illness define her, and she refused to let it steal her love for life. Her resilience reminded us all of her indomitable spirit and her unwavering will to fight for the people she loved.

Her final journey was both heartbreaking and beautiful. Wrapped in the simplicity and purity of white cloth, she looked peaceful, as though she had found eternal rest. We carried her memories, each step heavy with grief yet filled with love and gratitude for everything she had given us. At the Tower of Silence, as prayers rose to the heavens, we knew she had found her place among the stars, watching over us as she always had.

Her love was unconditional and unwavering, and her presence in my life was nothing short of a blessing. Though she is no longer here in body, her spirit lives on in the countless memories she left behind and in the love that continues to bind us all.

Rest well, Benu. You were, and always will be, our guiding light. Miss you sis!

Chapter 13: The White Elephant

The house stands tall, a relic of a bygone era, its grandeur weathered by time yet still commanding a quiet dignity. Built 116 years ago, it was designed for a world that no longer exists, a world of large families under one roof, where laughter echoed through its halls, every room bore witness to countless stories, and every corner held a secret, every drawer a forgotten relic waiting to be rediscovered.

Now, it feels like a white elephant. Majestic, beautiful, yet burdensome, it looms over our lives, its sheer scale and demands an ever-present shadow. The tiles, once gleaming, are now dulled and cracked, the walls peeling like parchment, whispering tales of generations who once lived here. The repairs feel endless, another leaky roof to fix, more crumbling plaster, yet another fault in the aging wiring. It's a constant tug-of-war between nostalgia and practicality, between the heart's longing and the mind's reality.

The attic, once a secret haven for childhood adventures, now feels like a forgotten relic of another time. Its slanted ceiling is a mosaic of cobwebs that glisten faintly in the light sneaking through a cracked skylight. The air is heavy with the musty smell of disuse, a cocktail of aged wood and forgotten memories. Dust blankets every surface like an unspoken agreement between time and neglect. Old trunks lie half-open, their latches rusted, revealing glimpses of yellowed letters tied in fraying ribbons and moth-eaten clothes that speak of a fashion long past. Each piece tells its own story, a lace shawl that once graced a grandmother's shoulders, a letter written in a careful, looping script, carrying whispers of love, regret, and hope.

Scattered among these treasures are toys, broken yet achingly familiar. A wooden spinning top, its colors faded, lies exactly where it was left, as if waiting for its owner to return.

The old outhouse, once bustling with activity, is now a crumbled shell, overtaken by nature's relentless march. The bricks, weathered and moss-covered, have given way in places. A rusted bucket sits in a corner, its handle long gone, while a cracked mirror still clings to the wall, its surface clouded but still hinting at reflections of a time when this space was alive with purpose.

As I walk through the quiet halls of this grand house, I often find myself asking: Are we right to keep it all going? Is it wise to pour so much of ourselves, our time, energy, and resources, into preserving a house when the world it was built for is fading with every passing day?

The drawers in the house are a treasure trove of discovery and decay. Opening one is an act of bravery, for it comes with a puff of dust that stings the eyes and tickles the nose. Inside, chaos reigns, a jumble of odds and ends that feel too precious to throw away yet too irrelevant to use. There are half-burned candles, their wax hardened into grotesque shapes, rusting scissors, and stray buttons of all colors and sizes. Amidst the clutter, forgotten gems emerge: an old photograph of a family picnic, the edges curling with age; a diary with entries written in an eager, youthful hand, now smudged and barely legible. Spiders have laid claim to the corners, their delicate webs laced with dust, while an army of ants patrols the wooden grooves, their presence a stark reminder that life persists, even in neglect.

The large cupboards in forgotten rooms hold history in their silence. Rows of clothes, some threadbare and others surprisingly intact, sway gently as the cupboard door creaks open. The smell of naphthalene mingles with that of old fabric, evoking a strange comfort. Here, too, the past refuses to let go. A sari with intricate embroidery catches the eye, its vibrant colors dulled but its beauty undiminished. Beneath the clothes lie shoes, their soles cracked, and a tin box holding trinkets that once meant everything to someone: an old wristwatch, its hands frozen in time; a necklace of wooden beads; and a coin from a year that no one remembers. These remnants, untouched for years, feel almost alive, as though holding their breath, waiting for someone to notice them again.

And notice them we do, for these small, forgotten treasures echo the vibrancy of a home that was once brimming with life. They lead us back to a time when the house was a hub of activity, a sanctuary for family and friends alike. It was home not just to us but to extended family, neighbors who dropped by without warning, and even the occasional stray dog that decided to make our garden its home.

The dining table, massive and welcoming, was always surrounded by laughter, arguments, and the clinking of plates. The garden, oh, the garden! was lush and alive, a playground for us as children and a backdrop for weddings, birthdays, and late-night conversations under the stars. Those cupboards, those trinkets, they remind us that even in silence, the house still hums with the memory of those lively days.
But now, the laughter has dimmed. The children have grown up and moved away. The echoes of the past seem louder than the faint stirrings of the present.

The garden is overgrown, its former glory buried under wild weeds and neglect. The house stands, quieter and emptier, a monument to a world that feels increasingly distant.

And yet, for all its burdens, it's not just bricks and mortar. It's a vessel of memory, a silent witness to our family's triumphs and trials. This is where my great-grandparents laid the foundation of their lives, where my parents dreamed and toiled, and where we, as children, imagined futures that seemed limitless.

These questions haunt me, lingering like the scent of old wood and faded flowers that fills its rooms. But they also ground me. This house, in its quiet, commanding way, reflects the tension between holding on and letting go, between honoring heritage and embracing change. For now, it remains. A white elephant, yes, but also a guardian of our family's story. Whether it stands for another century or becomes a cherished chapter in our collective memory, it will always be more than just a house. It will be home, our home, standing tall at 116 years, weathered but unbroken, a testament to all the lives it has held and the love it has sheltered.

Chapter 14: A Memory Preserved

Every story must come to an end and so must this one. Writing this book has been a journey of love, reflection, and remembrance. It is not merely a collection of anecdotes and memories; it is a piece of my soul poured into these pages. This book is my attempt to capture the essence of our family, the house that shaped us, the people who defined us, and the stories that bind us together. It is my way of preserving the laughter, the tears, the traditions, and the bonds that make us who we are.

This is the first of many books I have written so far, each about my memories and ideas of you. This is my first-ever try at writing a book, but there are many more to come.

The truth is the reason behind writing this book is deeply personal. It is not about fame or money; it is about creating something that transcends time. It all began in 2018 when I was studying in Canada. Out of curiosity, I decided to take a DNA test through "MyHeritage". I wanted to know where we came from, to trace our roots, and perhaps understand more about the history woven into our being.

What I discovered was unexpected. Along with learning about my ancestral roots, the test revealed that I am at a high risk of developing Alzheimer's disease. For those unfamiliar, Alzheimer's is a progressive neurological condition that affects memory, thinking, and behavior. Over time, it causes one to lose the ability to remember people, places, and even oneself. This revelation was unsettling, not just because of the implications for my future, but also because it brought back the stories of my grandfather.

He too had Alzheimer's, and the slow but inevitable toll it took on him and everyone who loved him. The thought of walking the same path was daunting.

That was when I decided to write this book. I knew that if the day ever came when I began to forget the faces of those I hold dear, I would want something to bring it all back, a tangible reminder of the people and moments that define my life. This book is my anchor to the memories that matter most.
I have tried to capture everything here: the warmth of our home, the strength of our family, and the beauty of the bonds we share. I wrote this book so that one day, when my mind might fail me, my heart won't. These pages will help me relive the cherished moments, the love, and the laughter we've shared.

Even if I forget your faces, your voices, or your presence, this book will be my guide back to you. And one day, as time takes its inevitable toll, there might come a moment when the vividness of my memories starts to blur. I might forget the taste of Mahrukh Kaki's rum cake, that perfect blend of sweetness and warmth that feels like a hug on a plate. Or the way Rati Kaki makes her eggs and those special baked dishes that she always prepared just for me with so much love.

There may be a day when I no longer remember how Benu cared for me, with her quiet strength and unwavering kindness, or the way Yasu's laughter could light up even the gloomiest of days. I might not recall how Sanaya shows her love in her own unique, gentle way or the mischievous sparkle in Delara's eyes right before she pulls off one of her legendary pranks.

These details, the little threads that weave the fabric of our shared history, may one day slip from my grasp, lost to the relentless march of time.

———

But if that day comes, I hope you can find it in your hearts to forgive me. Please know that my forgetting is not a choice or a lack of love; it is a cruel trick of fate, a betrayal of my own mind. Because even if the names, the faces, and the voices grow distant in my memory, my heart will never stop loving each one of you with every ounce of its being.

Even in forgetting, I will carry you all with me, etched into the deepest recesses of my soul where no disease, no distance, no passage of time can ever reach. My love for you is not tied to memory alone; it is a part of who I am, of what makes me whole. This book is my anchor to all of you, a way to hold on when my mind may falter, a testament to the bond we share that no force can erase.

So, if there comes a day when my gaze feels distant, when my words stumble over the names I've cherished for a lifetime, please understand that it isn't because you've been forgotten. Instead, it's a sign that my mind has turned traitor, but my love remains steadfast and unyielding. And in those moments, I hope you will find comfort in these pages, a piece of me that remembers everything, that celebrates every laugh, every tear, every shared meal, and every heartfelt moment.

This book is my promise to you all, a promise that no matter how much time passes, or how much my mind may betray me, the love I hold for you will remain unbroken and eternal.

I think about Polly Kaka's wit and wisdom, Rati Kaki's quiet strength, and the unspoken love they've shown me over the years. I think about Mahrukh Kaki's nurturing spirit, her dhai chawal that always tasted like comfort, and Dad's unwavering support as a brother.

I think about mom, who has always been there with her warm, gentle smile, and Mehernosh kaka, who could light up any room with his infectious laughter.

I think about my sisters, Benaifer, Yasmin, Sanaya, and Delara. Each of whom has left an indelible mark on my life. Together, we've shared countless moments of joy and sorrow, and I've tried to weave those memories into these pages. If Alzheimer's ever tries to steal them away from me, I'll have this book to remind me of who they are and what they mean to me. I think about the house that was not just a shelter but a sanctuary. It was where traditions were upheld, where laughter echoed through the halls, and where every corner held a story waiting to be told. From the kitchen filled with the aroma of Tulsi Bai's cooking to the verandah where we sat sharing cups of chai, that house is a part of who we are.

And I think about myself, Kerfegar. I am the youngest of the family, the shy and quiet one, but with a heart full of love for everyone around me. Writing this book has been a way to express that love, to put into words what I often find difficult to say out loud. This book is more than just a collection of stories; it is a promise. It is my way of saying that no matter what happens, I will never truly forget you.

And if, one day, you find me sitting quietly with a distant look in my eyes, please know that it is not because I don't love you, it is because my mind has betrayed me. But this book will remain, a testament to the love I have for each of you.

For me, this book is my way of holding on. It is my love letter to this family, this house, and this life. And even if my mind fades, my heart will always remember.

<hr>